BORN IN 1974?
WHAT ELSE HAPPENED?

PUBLISHED BY BOOM BOOKS
www.boombooks.biz

ABOUT THIS SERIES

.... But after that, I realised that I knew very little about these parents of mine. They had been born about the start of the Twentieth Century, and they died in 1970 and 1980. For their last 50 years, I was old enough to speak with a bit of sense.

I could have talked to them a lot about their lives. I could have found out about the times they lived in. But I did not. I know almost nothing about them really. Their courtship? Working in the pits? The Lock-out in the Depression? Losing their second child? Being dusted as a miner? The shootings at Rothbury? My uncles killed in the War? Love on the dole? There were hundreds, thousands of questions that I would now like to ask them. But, alas, I can't. It's too late.

Thus, prompted by my guilt, I resolved to write these books. They describe happenings that affected people, real people. The whole series is, to coin a modern phrase, designed to push your buttons, to make you remember and wonder at things forgotten.

The books might just let nostalgia see the light of day, so that oldies and youngies will talk about the past and re-discover a heritage otherwise forgotten. Hopefully, they will spark discussions between generations, and foster the asking and answering of questions that should not remain unanswered.

BORN IN 1974?
WHAT ELSE HAPPENED?

RON WILLIAMS

AUSTRALIAN SOCIAL HISTORY

BOOK 36 IN A SERIES OF 36

FROM 1939 to 1974

War Babies Years (1939 to 1945): 7 Titles
Baby Boom Years (1946 to 1960): 15 Titles
Post Boom Years (1961 to 1974): 14 Titles

BOOM, BOOM BABY, BOOM

BORN IN 1974? WHAT ELSE HAPPENED?
Published by Boom Books
Wickham, NSW, Australia

Web: www.boombooks.biz
Email: jen@boombooks.biz

Creator: Williams, Ron, 1934- author.

Title: Born in 1974? What else happened?

ISBN: 9780645182651

Subjects: Australia, History, Miscellanea--20th Century.

From the collection of the National Archives of Australia:
A6135 K7/2/74/22 Research - Astronomy and space
A6135 K14/11/74/27 Fishing - Brramundi caught for record and tagging Mary River NT
A6135 K17/9/74/7 Horses at Randwick early morning training
A6135 K20/2/74/6 Miss Australia Honey at Adelaide Uni

TABLE OF CONTENTS

SOME IMPORTANT PEOPLE AND EVENTS

Queen of Britain	Elizabeth II
PM of Oz	Gough Whitlam
Opposition Leader	William M Snedden
Governor General - till July	Paul Hasluck
- after July	Sir John Kerr
The Pope	Paul VI
US President - till August	Richard Nixon
- after August	Gerald Ford
PM of Britain - till March	Edward Heath
- after March	Harold Wilson

WINNER OF ASHES

1970 - 71	England 2 - 0
1972	Draw 2 - 2
1974 -75	Australia 4 - 1

WINNERS OF MELBOURNE CUP

1973	Gala Supreme
1974	Think Big

ACADEMY AWARDS, 1974

Best Actor	Jack Lemon
Best Actress	Glenda Jackson
Best Movie	The Sting

INTRODUCTION TO THIS SERIES

This book is the 36th in a series of books that I have researched and written. It tells a story about a number of important or newsworthy Australia-centric events that happened in 1974. The series covers each of the 36 years from 1939 to 1974, for a total of 36 books.

I developed my interest in writing these books a few years ago at a time when my children entered their teens. My own teens started in 1947, and I started trying to remember what had happened to me then. I thought of the big events first, like Saturday afternoon at the pictures, and cricket in the back yard, and the wonderful fun of going to Maitland on the train for school each day. Then I recalled some of the not-so-good things. I was an altar boy, and that meant three or four Masses a week. I might have thought I loved God at that stage, but I really hated his Masses. And the schoolboy bullies, like Greg Favell, and the hapless Freddie Bevan. Yet, to compensate for these, there was always the beautiful, black headed, blue-sailor-suited June Browne, who I was allowed to worship from a distance.

I also thought about my parents. Most of the major events that I lived through came to mind readily. But after that, I realised that I really knew very little about these parents of mine. They had been born about the start of the Twentieth Century, and they died in 1970 and 1980. For their last 20 years, I was old enough to speak with a bit of sense. I could have talked to them a lot about their lives. I could have found out about the times they lived in.

But I did not. I know almost nothing about them really. Their courtship? Working in the pits? The Lock-out in the Depression? Losing their second child? Being dusted as a miner? The shootings at Rothbury? My uncles killed in the War? There were hundreds, thousands of questions that I would now like to ask them. But, alas, I can't. It's too late.

Thus, prompted by my guilt, I resolved to write these books. They describe happenings that affected people, real people. In 1974, there is some coverage of international affairs, but a lot more on social events within Australia. This book, and the whole series is, to coin a modern phrase, designed to push the reader's buttons, to make you remember and wonder at things forgotten. The books might just let nostalgia see the light of day, so that oldies and youngies will talk about the past and re-discover a heritage otherwise forgotten. Hopefully, they will spark discussions between generations, and foster the asking and the answering of questions that should not remain unanswered.

The sources of my material. I was born in 1934, so that I can remember well a great deal of what went on around me from 1939 onwards. But of course, the bulk of this book's material came from research. That meant that I spent many hours in front of a computer reading electronic versions of newspapers, magazines, Hansard, Ministers' Press releases and the like. My task was to sift out, day-by-day, those stories and events that would be of interest to the most readers. Then I supplemented these with materials from books, broadcasts, memoirs, biographies, government reports and statistics. And I talked to old-timers, one-on-one, and in organised groups, and to Baby Boomers and post Baby Boomers about their recollections. People with stories to tell came out of the woodwork, and talked no end about the tragic and funny and commonplace events that have shaped their lives.

The presentation of each book. For each year, the end result is a collection of Chapters on many of the topics that concerned ordinary people in that year. I think I have covered most of the major issues that people then were interested in. On the other hand, in some cases I have dwelt a little on minor frivolous matters, perhaps to the detriment of more sober considerations. Still, in the long run, this makes the book more readable, and hopefully it will convey adequately the spirit of the times.

I have been deliberately national in outlook, so that readers elsewhere in Australia will feel comfortable that I am talking about matters that affected them personally. After all, housing shortages, and strikes, and juvenile delinquency involved **all** Australians, and other issues, such as problems overseas, had no State component in them.

Overall, I expect I can make you wonder, remember, rage and giggle equally, no matter where you hail from. Here though, in the short run, I will start by presenting some background material from the year 1973 that should get you started.

START OF THE WHITLAM LEGACY

In December of 1972, Gough Whitlam led the Labor Party to a resounding victory in the national elections. He increased the number of seats that he held so that in the Lower House, he could do whatever he liked.

But in the Senate, that was not the case. The Liberals had enough Senators who survived retirement, and that meant that Whitlam and his Ministers always had some measure of restraint on their enthusiasm.

Still, **enthusiasm among the Government was unbounded**. It had been in Opposition for over twenty years, with all the frustrations and disappointments that came with this. But now, it was in power. The new Ministers were a tough lot, **ready** for a fight, hardened, and they were **ready** to make the world a better place with their plans for a better Australia. Each of them thought, there is only one way forward, and that way is mine.

By the time they were actually in office, in early 1973, they were ready to **change**. For example, Whitlam himself was a great advocate of universally-welcome adjustments to **the divorce laws**. The entire nation suffered under laws, which had been around for decades, that made the granting of a divorce an agony for years for both parties. **Whitlam took the concept of fault out of all divorce settlements.** And he unified them across the nation. Property disputes in future were to be based on agreed principles, and **that** reduced the quagmire of settlements **down to the lower levels** of agony and chaos that still remain today.

Hundreds of other social changes were in the air. For example, **civil marriages** outside of churches were encouraged by new laws. The idea that they should be conducted only by churchmen, was now taboo. The celebrants indeed could now be women.

Internationally, **we were no longer worried by the war in Vietnam**. America had still not withdrawn many of its troops, and President Nixon was still to face the music for his involvement in **Watergate**. And, of course, the horror of resigning his office. But we were well out of all that controversy, and by the start of the year, we had settled down to our common state of letting the rest of the world go by un-noticed.

WHITLAM'S NEW ASIA POLICY

The two places in the world where we were active was in China and Japan. Prior to the election, the Liberal Government had a policy of distrust and muted animosity towards the Chinese. This was understandable enough given that we had been fighting them in Vietnam for a decade. But with Whitlam, all of this had gone. We started to trade with them, we exchanged trade missions with them, even Whitlam himself visited China. The Vietnam War? What war?

Likewise with Japan. Our old resentment, and sometimes hatred carrying over from WWII, was still there for many Australians. Most of us were happy to forgive, if nor forget.

But now, all things between the two nations were bright and beautiful. And needless to say, trade between the two countries benefited and thrived. World War II? What war?

WHITLAM'S POLITICS

He and his Cabinet were, every one of them, extreme political animals. They were obsessed with making the world a better place, but knew that they could do that only if they got elected again next time. So they all had their eyes on the political clock, and their thoughts on how to attract voters to their flock.

Whitlam hit on a powerful tactic. He wooed the Commonwealth Public Service. In a series of gifts over 1973, he gave them salary increases, long service leave concessions, maternity leave, shorter working week. All for free. This was very popular with these Servants.

But the brilliance was that he knew that, given the maze of wage-fixing authorities that controlled all aspects of work, these benefits would flow into the State Public Services, then into local Governments. And from there, into private businesses. In short, into the pockets of all wage and salary earners. **And all for the measly sum paid to the Commonwealth Servants.** Great thinking.

The end result for Whitlam was that by the start of 1974, he was still enthusiastically supported by the bulk of the population. People were still excited by the changes that were being proposed and implemented. They still believed in the Whitlam election slogan, IT'S TIME, and were quite ready to give Whitlam, and his team, more bites at the cherry.

MINOR MATTERS

Other events in 1973 came and went. Fluoridation of water supply hit the headlines for while. Our new currency was no longer called Shillings and Pence, but Dollars and Cents. The Churches collectively were getting further away from their flocks, and were doing little to rectify this. The States were fighting different battles against bookies, and trying to promote their own TABs as a legal substitute.

The murder of Bogle and Chandler was still a topic of conversation, as was the growing delinquency of teenagers. The elderly were still short-changed, but that was to be expected and no one cared. Until it was their turn. We rejected the suggestion that large numbers of American blacks be encouraged to migrate here. All people complained about the food services provided on our trains. But this was easily fixed by the Railways. They stopped providing them.

Our Aborigines were now allowed to enter and drink in hotels. There were many people advocating that nuclear power be used to create weapons for use against enemies, and for electrical power. A lady complained that her concert had been spoiled by another lady who had been knitting loudly.

NOTES FOR READERS

First note,   Throughout this book, I rely a lot on reproducing Letters from the newspapers. Whenever I do this, I put the text in a different font, and indent it a little, and make the font somewhat smaller. I do not edit the text at all. That is, I do not correct spelling or grammar. If the text gets at all garbled, I do not change it. It's just as it was seen in the Papers of the day.

Second note. The material for this book, when it comes from newspapers, is reported as it was seen at the time. If the benefit of hindsight over the years changes things, then I might record that in Comments. The info reported thus reflects matters as they were seen in 1974.

Third note. Let me also apologise in advance to anyone I might offend. In a work such as this, it is certain some people will think I got some things wrong. I am sure that I did, but please remember, **all of this is only my opinion**. And really, **my opinion does not matter one little bit in the scheme of things**. I hope you will say "silly old bugger", and shrug your shoulders and keep reading on.

So, now, 1974, here we come.

JANUARY NEWS ITEMS

The Queen's New Years Honours list always fills me with awe. How could it be that there were so many truly distinguished Australians out there that I have never heard of....

But one recipient of a Knighthood I **had** heard of. **Fletcher Jones**, was a well-known name because he was always associated with providing gentlemen's suits. At a time when every man had **one** best suit, Fletcher Jones was the one to strut in....

He came from a poor beginning and hawked his way around Australia for years, until he entered the clothing business. And now **this humble man is Sir Fletcher**.

Two professors at Tokyo University have developed a process that **makes hydrogen fuel from water**. This, as you know, will be non-polluting, and even at a time when pollution was not seen as much of a problem, was a significant break-through....

Pity that, 50 years later, we have seen no commercial development of this game-changer. **I wonder why not.**

The President of France, M. Pompidou, announced that his nation would continue with **their N-bomb tests in the Pacific**. This was despite protests from Australian Trade Unions, New Zealand the Pacific nations, and half the world.

A 14-year old boy was killed yesterday in a Melbourne beachside suburb. A gust of wind whipped the umbrella from over a table, and it hit the boy behind his ear. **It killed him instantly.**

Several experts agreed that the only recognised **fashion for men in Australia was shorts with long socks.**

Australian Teachers Federation decided to **ban the use of the cane, and straps, in schools.** These instruments had been widely used to maintain discipline. Especially in boys' schools, and in private schools.

Hoover Australia has announced **a product-recall for 45,000 of its vacuum cleaners.** This followed the death of one person, and the injuries of two others in the last week. The incidents were associated with the self-assembly of the product....

This was reported as the **largest recall of a product in Australia to date.**

A woman in South Africa got her name into the world's record books by **giving birth to six babies,** all of which survived and are doing well.

Charles Perkins, **one of the first Aboriginals to graduate from an Australian University,** commented on recent riots involving Aboriginals in Australia's north. He said that the problem was not the excessive consumption of alcohol, but poor housing conditions....

Comment. Have things changed in the last 50 years?

GETTING SLOWLY OFF THE GROUND

!974 got off to a slow start. This surprised no one, because every year started this way. **Most of the population was on holiday.** City folk had moved to the country or beaches, and country folk had moved to the cities or beaches. It was nice to get away from the daily routine and problems, and forget the mortgage, the irritations of Councils, the worries about children, or surviving on the pension. Instead, people could have barbecues, listen to the cricket and tennis, and play a lot of board games, with the occasional beer and reminiscence. Forget the horror headlines. Sit and daydream, and plan what you will do better this coming year.

The newspapers too were on holidays. The editions were slimmer, their ambitious alarmist journalists and editors had slowed down to a trot, and headlines were not as frightening.

So, nicely, lesser news, for a month, filled the pages. Letters were printed that ranged from trivial to very trivial, and the ordinary Aussie had a voice for a little while.

So, I will start the year with a selection of Letters on matters that were commonplace, and that would never otherwise have seen the light of day.

NOISY PEOPLE

Letters, D Condon. In these days of fairly cheap transistor radios it seems to me to be unnecessary to broadcast radio programs over loudspeakers at the beach.

Most people would be careful about foisting their own taste in radio listening onto somebody else.

At Coogee Beach, for example, the equipment being used to amplify these broadcasts has a high degree of distortion and, content apart, is unpleasant to the ear.

Noise pollution in the community is an ever-increasing problem. Those responsible for these broadcasts would do well to reconsider their contribution.

In plain words, could we have some peace and quiet when we visit the beach?

Comment. By now, in the twenty-twenties years, this irritation has been stopped on most beaches. But for a long period it was a real menace. I cannot remember when it went away, but I recall that in the year 2010, I went to a Sydney beach, and the so-called music almost spoiled the day for me.

CANES IN SCHOOL

Letters, (Mrs) C Claasz. Mr B Francis quite rightly believes that the use of the cane in schools is negative, rather than positive, punishment.

As a teacher, however, I feel it necessary to point out that as long as parents continue to mete out corporal punishment as the sole form of sanction at home, it is that same form of sanction which will be the most clearly understood, and therefore the most effective at school, in certain circumstances.

Comment. The use of canes in schools was still a hot issue.

PLASTIC POLLUTION

Letters, (Mrs) P Howard. At a time when concern for our environment is supposedly foremost in everyone's minds, why are table margarine manufacturers turning to plastic containers (tubs) for all sizes of margarine?

Surely it is obvious that these plastic containers do not decompose and, as far as I know, cannot be recycled. They generally end up dumped in large numbers at the local council tip, together with many other wasteful and non-reusable packaging containers also obtained in the first instance from supermarkets.

There must be better ways of "packaging" than this short-term method. Environmental concern must be practised, not just talked about, for everyone's benefit.

I hope that at least one of the manufacturers of table margarine will take the initiative and come up with a simple and practical "environmentally conscious" method of packaging to replace the plastic tub. I'm sure other margarine manufacturers would then follow on in the interests of the entire community.

Comment. These were early days for environmentalists, and this was one of the earliest Letters to be published on the dangers of plastic.

But, more generally the environmental movement was only at its birth. There were lots of passionate people who were ready to fight for their causes, but they had not yet welded into a coherent voice. So voices such as Pam Howard's were scarcely heard, and it was not until the opposition to environment matters became organised that it became effective.

For example, in the building industry, leaders like Trade Unionist Jack Mundey had, by now, imposed Green Bans on dozens of major building projects in the Eastern States.

MUNDEY AS AN ANGEL

Jack Mundey was a Communist and that gave him a bad name for most of the population. But he had the gift of the gab, and was able to present a good argument for his cause.

He said that he was acting on behalf of the common people to preserve buildings of historical significance from destruction by the hordes of developers. What **they** wanted to do was to knock down everything, and build towers that were higher and more lucrative for themselves. **Forget history, where's the money?**

I provide below an idea of his copious writings, and his obvious virtue.

Letters, J Mundey. Certainly, an owner of a historical building should be adequately compensated, but it should be remembered that for posterity **the building is substantially more important than any particular owner**.

Such an owner should not be presented with unnecessary bonuses, when one considers that in the Sydney central business district by mid-1974 at least eight million square metres of office space will stand idle.

With this in mind, how tragic it is that the Royal Australasian College of Physicians would entertain the idea of removing historic Stawell House, Macquarie Street (built in the 1840s), and re-erecting, it in the Rocks.

The character, charm and diversity of any city are bound up, to no small degree, in the city's ability to retain the finest buildings of various periods, and to retain them **where they were built**.

It is less than two years ago that a developer-orientated suggestion was advanced to remove **all** of Sydney's old historic buildings and rebuild them in a tourist park on the central coast! This led me to write to you on that outrageous "Coney Island" concept, which met with strong public opposition.

Alderman Port and Alderman Briger claim to want to breathe new life into the City. They won't do that by supporting the RACP and its myopic decision to pull down and transfer Stawell House.

I would like to remind the RACP, Mr G Brodie, "a director of Marayong Developments" who aims to demolish the home of Dr George Busby in Bathurst (built in 1836), and other friendly developers, that **the Builders Labourers' Federation** at its national conference, resolved to **"refuse to demolish any historical or architecturally significant building throughout Australia**, and call upon all Governments to immediately enact legislation to protect these buildings and ensure that these buildings remain part of our heritage."

This resolution was carried unanimously, and I am sure that it not only has the support of all thinking Australians, but that our action in refusing to demolish these buildings will hasten the necessary legislation and its early introduction.

No doubt the National Estate and the various National Trusts must support our positive and progressive action.

Comment. Surely, a man with such a sensible approach to conservation should be lauded, not criticised.

JANUARY   9

MUNDEY AS A DEVIL

But not everyone saw him so kindly. In fact, most people were convinced that he was the architect of anarchy in the building industry and was blocking progress, and much-needed renovation, in our Eastern cities. He was accused of controlling gangs of "Union Officials" who visited building sites and bashed workers and intimidated them until they walked off the job. And stayed off, often for months, sometimes for years. "Green bans" were placed on the site. Sometimes the building project was abandoned forever. He was also accused of extracting lucrative bribes from developers to lift their bans.

In all, the word "anarchy" was endlessly used to describe the state of the building industry. As for Mundey himself, he remained a powerful force in the industry, and in Australian life, until he was forced from his various offices around 1980. He still has his admirers among conservationists. Some of these regard him as the patron Saint, not because of his obstruction of the building industry, but because he taught environmentalists the value of **organised resistance through a body corporate**, rather than through individuals.

SCHOOL MILK

Letters, (Mrs) B Phelps, Gwabegar Mothers' Club. I would like to point out the obvious need of the small, remote primary schools for a continued supply of school milk. Isolated country schools, particularly in the western area, do not have a ready supply of milk, nor do

the pupils have daily and abundant amounts
of milk to drink.

In spite of the picture conjured in one's mind
when "country" is mentioned, this does not
imply that all areas and inhabitants have fresh
cow's milk ad lib.

On the contrary, many people in the country
and in country towns use powdered milk, and
it was only too obvious what happened during
recent railway freight-handling stoppages - the
milk supply was curtailed, for there was little
or no powdered milk on store shelves.

Our own local school has received bottled milk
during 1973, for the first time in my memory,
and that only because we had teachers
travelling daily from a larger town where supply
was delivered.

Before that, milk would have travelled
irregularly from Tamworth to Narrabri, Wee
Waa, Pilliga and thence to Gwabegar, before a
child received it - and then what state would it
have been in?

There are many large families living in
substandard conditions with many children
being deprived of essential foods for healthy
nutrition. The daily bottle of school milk at
least supplemented a restricted diet to a small
degree.

I foresee many children getting nothing to
take the place of this. I therefore urge a closer

appraisal of needy areas, and the reintroduction of milk where necessary.

Comment. Free school milk for primary schools was a mixed blessing. For health-conscious mothers, it was a welcome addition to the nutrition that their children got. For milk marketers is was a big boost to their fortunes. For corner retailers it was a curse, because they sold less milk over the counter.

For children, there were occasions, **rare occasions**, when it was at the right temperature, and had not sat in the sun since the milko delivered it at dawn. Sometimes the little bottles had not coagulated cream at the top, as unhomogenised milk does after a while. In some parts of some seasons in some regions, the temperature was hot enough that a cool drink of milk was welcome.

But, in most places and times, school children did not like the milk, and despite all sorts of urgings, finessed their way out of drinking it.

Second comment. I sometimes wonder whether it did in fact have any benefits. Or I wonder, at my age, whether I would have died sooner (or later) if I had swallowed it regularly. Or maybe, all that business about it was "good for you", was dubious?

I will leave that as a question for you to answer when you make up your mind.

BOUNCING BALLS

Letters, A D'Ombrain. I have been wondering if this ball-bouncing by nearly every tennis player when about to serve does anything to the player in the way of some sort of help.

I can't see what good it does, and mostly it is rather irritating to watch. I saw one top-class player do no fewer than seven bounces before making his serve in a big match during the last few days.

I have not played tennis myself for some years, but cannot remember any of the players carrying out this rather time-and-muscle-wasting effort.

I have watched tennis since the days of Norman Brookes, Gerald Patterson, the late J O Anderson and others of that time, and cannot see any really vast difference in the services compared with those of today's players.

II would like to see someone put a stopwatch on this bouncy business during a five-set match and find out how much time it takes up. Perhaps some of the top players can come up with some reason for it, but to me it seems rather unnecessary, and must use up some amount of muscular power.

Comment. The reader is perhaps too young to remember the years of World War II . Tennis then was a popular sport, and most towns in the nation had a few ant-bed courts to their credit. But the problem was that it was impossible to buy tennis balls anywhere, because of wartime restrictions. So the remaining stock had to be carefully husbanded to keep the game alive. One way of doing this was to keep the player from bouncing the ball before serving.

Tennis players all over the nation argued whether it should be a complete ban, or simply **a restriction perhaps to two bounces.** And argued about what penalties would be imposed on those who breached the limit. It finished only when the Associations said that no rules would be imposed, but it highly recommended that players abstain from the dreadful habit.

Of course, like many of the war-time regulations, no one took any notice, so the games continued with balls that got progressively hairless.

PUNCH-UPS ON THE HILL

A good-humored Letter from Mr Lee of London recounted how he went to the Sydney Cricked Ground to watch the cricket. Sitting on the Hill among friends, he was hit by an empty beer bottle, thrown from behind him. **No one around him seemed at all perturbed by this, and he asked if this was normal at Australian cricket.**

Letters, B Potts. Many of us who attended the Test match at the Sydney Cricket Ground on Sunday, when poor Mr Lee was crowned by a bottle, were staggered by *Column 8's* praise of the Hill crowd. My own reaction, and that of many around me, to Sunday's performance was one of disgust and shame.

If this sort of thing is to be praised and encouraged, it will become the regular pattern and a lot of people are going to get hurt. It was a scene of drunken caterwauling, and fights, fusillades of cans and bottles (many of which were aimed at police in the playing area).

Comments. The Hill at the Sydney Cricket Ground was once the epitome of Heaven. To be able to sit on green grass, with a few bottles of warm beer, a few mates and pretty girls, with your shirt off getting grossly sunburnt, was a wonderful experience never to be missed. And there was always the cricket too, quite often interesting.

Alas, **Jack Mundey was asleep**, and he let re-development of the Hill happen. Gradually, since about 1960, more grandstands have been added around the Ground, and much of it has been at the expense of the Hill. So, the green sward is all but gone,

As for the unsuspecting Pom who got hit by the beer bottle, pity for him. But had he known, that was always to be expected on the old Hill. Rarely on a hot Saturday afternoon did the day go by without some form of punch-up or two. And mass police charges, with linked arms, down the Hill through the crowd to get to the battle scene.

Alas, we now have only respectful civility on the skerrick of land that they now call the Hill. **What a pity.**

Where was Jack when we needed him?

FEBRUARY NEWS ITEMS

Delivery of mail to homes and businesses **on Saturdays** will cease from next weekend. 6,300 postmen and women will be pleased. But no one else.

An advertisement in a country newspaper read "FOR SALE. **Beautiful wedding gown SSW, never worn.** Also a two-tier wedding cake...."

Several Ministers in Western Australia are supportive of a suggestion that the wives of prisoners in gaols there should be allowed to visit on Saturdays and **stay the night with their husband....**

Comment. This suggestion was never adopted, even though there was a small but vocal group that supported it. They argued that **it would help in rehabilitation of prisoners on release.**

The **Great Train Robber, Ronald Biggs**, **was arrested** at a Rio de Janero hotel. This was the man who, with 14 others, robbed the Glasgow-to-London mail train, and escaped with 2.6 million Pounds. That was in 1963....

The entire gang was captured and gaoled, but **Biggs escaped in 1965**, at which time he still had 28 years to serve in prison. During his long period on the run, he had lived the high life all over the world, and was reported many times as being seen in Australia.

A riot at the prison in the NSW city of Bathurst destroyed the prison and injured 12 persons, all of whom were taken to hospital. At the start of the riot, petrol bombs were exploded at four different locations within the walls, and the flames quickly spread....

Most of those injured were **hit by pellets** that were fired into walls, and ricocheted into them. All of the 230 prisoners were transferred to Long Bay and Goulburn Gaols. Many of them were serving life sentences....

In the aftermath, there were many claims that **brutality by the warders was the cause**. As a result, a Royal Commission was ordered into the event. The aim was not primarily to examine the riot, but to study the many weaknesses in the treatment of prisoners.

A bus-load of 38 "old people" came off the road and overturned near Tumut, NSW. It tumbled down a slope of 300 metres, and plunged into a dam. **Eighteen of them were killed.** Brake failure was blamed.

In San Francisco, **Patricia Hurst was kidnapped.** She was the daughter of Randolph Hurst, extremely rich and controller of many newspapers....

She was dragged from her home, screaming, by two black men and a girl. Two days later, **the kidnappers had not made contact to demand ransom**.

The Prime Minister of Australia, Gough Whitlam, decided to **allow 35 semi-skilled Philipino** auto workers, and their families, **to enter Australia and work** for a sponsoring company.....

This was historic because it signalled that this nation would relax, and eventually **remove, its White Australia Policy,** which banned the permanent entry of Asians and others into Australia.

ENERGY ARGUMENTS

Letters, N Hutchison. The proposal by Congressman Craig Hosmer **to dump here the atomic waste of American nuclear reactors** is an impertinence of the worst order.

If anything will ever cause a break in the friendship between Australia and the United States, it will be just such a display of overriding self-interest.

Hasn't Mr Hosmer heard of solar energy? It does not pollute.

Letters, R Woollett, L Port. Your writer, A Young, is right in rejecting steam-propelled motor cars, but he is surely behind the times in suggesting the reintroduction of the horse and dray for delivery of milk and other perishables.

He will surely recall the swarms of flies which polluted in the horse dung, 40 years ago on the streets of Sydney, especially in hot weather.

Melbourne may still be using horses to deliver milk in the outer suburbs, but increasing use is being made of battery-electric milk floats in the inner suburbs. These electric milk floats are almost silent, and do not suffer from the carburetion problems occurring when internal combustion engines start and stop every 20 yards.

Sydney's milk vendors should follow Melbourne's lead in this.

Letters, J Carrick, Senator for NSW. Federal Government statements regarding Australia's oil supplies are thoroughly misleading and dangerously complacent.

It is true that present local production meets 70 per cent of our overall requirements (including the whole of our gasoline demands), and that our reliance on imports is essentially for the heavier industrial crudes.

Unfortunately, it is equally true that unless we discover new wells of equal capacity to the existing Bass Strait drillings, we will meet only 45 per cent of our needs by 1980 and less than 10 per cent by 1990.

In the face of these facts, there should have been **a major concentration on oil exploration during 1973** and a "crash" program devised for those years immediately ahead. The reverse is true. Due to the **Federal Government's withdrawal of exploration incentives**, 1973 has been the worst year for oil drilling for more than a decade, and the prospects for 1974 are even more dismal.

To meet this critical challenge, annual exploration expenditure of at least $200 million is necessary, rising to $300 million. The present level of investment is $80 million. There have been no major oil discoveries in Australia since 1969.

The position will not be resolved by doctrinaire socialist techniques or by blustering and inveighing against the oil companies. The creation and distortion of the multi-national bogyman can be no substitute for a rational energy policy.

The oil companies have immense resources and know-how, which should be encouraged to work in our national interest. The BHP-Esso enterprise has shown dramatically that this can be done.

Personal Comment. The arguments over which form of energy to use have been round for a long time. The cry from Senator Carrick for a national energy policy can still be recognised 50 years later.

By then, the arguments might remain as futile as they ever were, **but** the situation has got even more confusing. Technology and changing knowledge have introduced solar energy, and wind power, and tidal power into the equation. As well as nuclear energy in all Western countries, except Australia. **There are more options now available.**

But we are still confronted with the enigma that Australia has **more natural sources of energy** than any other nation in the world, and **yet** we still lack a generally accepted national policy on what to do with it.

I hope, and I am sure you do too, that some day soon we can think our way to the happy state where there are no blackouts, and that people can boil the jug without worrying about the cost.

MARGARET WHITLAM

Margaret was the wife of our Prime Minister. She was a University graduate with good scholastic achievements, and had a fine work record that included being a Social Worker.

She was now offered a Directorship on the Board of Commonwealth Hostels. This carried a small stipend.

With her experience and intelligence, this would seem to be a normal offer, given that women were, at the time, being promoted to many such positions.

But, life is not that simple. There were many people who objected, saying that here we had another classic example of Whitlam giving **jobs to the girls**, and of Margaret being all sorts of greedy imposter.

The correspondence on her appointment varied from condemnation to wild support.

Letters, J Lindsay. If Mrs Whitlam is serious in her declaration that she is not interested in the financial side of her appointment to the board of Commonwealth Hostels Ltd - how about an equally public declaration as to which charity she plans to donate her salary to.

Letters, (Mrs) R Whitfield. What has happened to all the Women's Lib supporters that they are not coming to the defence of Mrs Whitlam? Surely she has the right, and obviously the wish, to do her own thing, and put her training and experience to use in some worthwhile avenues, rather than just opening bazaars or appearing on platforms merely in a social capacity.

No doubt the type of work she does will have some influence on how she spends the money.

Letters, B Baxter. Poor Mrs Whitlam! How sad that she cannot make ends meet on her husband's annual pittance of $56,000 provided by the tight-fisted taxpayer, and now has to add to the arduous duty of peddling piffle to women's magazines by shouldering aside other, probably more qualified, Social Workers in order to obtain a job. The heart of every honest taxpayer must be bleeding for her today.

Letters, L Gilmore. Congratulations on your excellent editorial, "Jobs for the girls". If Mrs Whitlam has time to take on extra work, she is evidently not doing her job as the Prime Minister's wife. It seems to me that she wants all the perks of public life without the sometimes necessary boredom.

Perhaps Mr Whitlam should be given a rise in wages, poor man, as apparently he cannot afford to keep his wife on his present meagre salary - just $56,500, including allowances, isn't it? My heart bleeds for him!

Letters, S Hislop. I hold no special brief for Mrs Whitlam, but thousands of working wives and professional married women, whatever their politics, will resent your petty attack on this respected and talented woman.

Perhaps the "Herald" would prefer that all social work were performed by an idle elite of do-gooders and charity ladies, seeking relief from the tedium of bridge parties.

At least they could afford to decline the salary. Nowadays we recognise that professional work requires professional workers, and that professional workers are entitled to be paid, **whoever their husbands or wives may be**.

Letters, D Richardson. I agree wholeheartedly with the principle of having a qualified woman on the Board of the Commonwealth Hostels.

There is no doubt many qualified women would have jumped at the chance to be in Mrs Whitlam's position with the Board.

One wonders why this appointment was not offered to one of them - especially as the salary of qualified senior social workers is quite poor, and the additional amount being paid for this job would have been very helpful.

Letters, (Mrs) D Jeffery. The people who are first housed in Commonwealth Hostels will welcome the appointment of a woman to the directorate - from what I have heard of these places, some are rather stark and comfortless.

Among the migrants housed there (including many children), there are at least 50 per cent members of Mrs Whitlam's sex - women! At last on a board of eight her influence can do only good.

Personal Comment. With the benefit of hindsight, Margaret Whitlam, now in the public spotlight, proved to be a very capable, interested, and sound advocate for justice, and the Australian Way, in her many public activities.

The duties that came with the Directorship were not onerous, and never interfered with her duties as wife to the Prime Minister.

I think that many writers who criticised her **now** would have changed their minds a couple of years later.

A BAN ON TOBACCO ADVERTISING

Letters, R Nicks, MS, FRCS, Royal Prince Alfred Hospital. I believe that Mr Whitlam would enjoy general public support if he were to ban all cigarette advertising.

The Labor Government places great emphasis on health measures for the prevention of serious illness and disease. **This is one!**

I am sure that the whole medical profession would support him if he were to see this in its true perspective and make a law binding throughout the Commonwealth.

Comment. Actually, a ban was placed on **advertising on radio** in 1971. But the money then went to magazines and **the print media.**

These bans may or may not been the cause of a reduction in tobacco usage over that period, but it seems that a bigger part of the reduction was the growing public awareness of the health dangers in smoking.

The penny was starting to drop.

OVERLOADING DOCTORS

Letters, (Dr) W Utber. Your informative articles of January 30 and 31 should leave your readers in no doubt about the long hours worked by Resident medical officers, and the arduous and responsible nature of their duties would not be doubted by anyone.

In times when emotional and irrational words are spoken by medical authorities, and by Government leaders, it would appear that now we are coming to the core of the matter. What is a man (or woman) worth for his services?

Maybe it will take a younger generation of Residents to bring sane thinking to the public regarding hours worked, services rendered and payment for such services.

Which section of the community works 100 hours or more for a salary not much more than the average?

The tradition of honorary services (no charge to the patient), prolonged working hours, 24-hour seven-day availability and respect for human nature is now an anachronism in days of 35-hour-a-week clamour, strikes by all and sundry, escalating inflation and denigration of the very principles that most of us try to preserve. In the face of such odds, it is hard to see clearly where we are heading.

The Residents have a good point. Eighteen years ago I was in the same position, working the same hours and paying half my salary in rent. If we had been militant then, perhaps conditions would be better now for both Residents and older graduates.

I now find that working 65 hours a week and 30 hours on call, together with responsibilities entailed in running the show, plus family and community commitments, leave me with little time to spend the wealth that people imagine I have.

The large influx of Indian and Asian Residents is a reflection on a laissez-faire attitude of our university authorities, who have left us with depleted ranks.

I suppose that in the long run, it is up to every one to make his own choice as to what path he takes. There is no guarantee that one will chose the right one.

Your articles are close to the nitty-gritty of truth in a complex and confused issue.

Comment. Many readers, especially tradesmen, claim to work longer hours in harder jobs for less pay and also bitterly claim to have had a hard time surviving apprentice pay. Wouldn't they like to get the pay that Utber gets.

Another chorus came from housewives. Writers claim to work longer hours, have decades without promotion, and get no pay at all.

Some writers agreed that there is a shortage of doctors, and hence high charges for their services. But they argue this shortage is caused by doctors themselves who place so many restrictions on permitting entry to practice.

Doctor Utber did not get much sympathy from Letter-writers.

DIRTY DAGOES

A number of Articles and Letters were written that made the sweeping claim that all Italians were dirty and unwashed and unhygenic. This was supposedly true in Italy and also for those whose adopted home was Australia.

Given the large numbers of Italians who had come here to live after WWI, and the masses who had migrated in the decade after WII, these writings got a lot of Italians, and their children, stirred up.

The Letter below is moderate, but carries the message.

Letters, (Mrs) L Beenleigh. In view of the reportedly low standard of hygiene in Italy, perhaps a compulsory crash course in personal and public hygiene should be a condition of entry of migrants from Italy to this country.

We are really importing a health hazard, considering the fact that so many Italians are attracted to the various food-handling-and-preparation type of work and shops.

It may be appropriate to mention that, a short drive from Rome, it is possible to view beautiful hillside fountains, all expensively floodlit - and to be startled by the whiff of raw sewage!

I have travelled extensively in many countries, with the maximum of health "shots," but Italy proved to be the only country where our family contracted what is vaguely termed "food poisoning."

The response below is typical.

Letters, (Mrs) F Arena. It is letters like that of Mrs L Beenleigh that sometimes make me despair, not only about the future of Australia but of the world.

Please take note of the prejudices still existing, how strong they still are. Mrs Beenleigh thinks that we Italians might be a health hazard.

Every year more than 20 million tourists visit beautiful Italy, and that very few of them get poisoned by our way of life. I am sorry that the smell of sewage disturbed you while you were looking at Roman fountains; perhaps you have never been outside our beautiful Sydney Heads and seen the raw sewage there. But of course Sydney has a lot to teach the world regarding sewage; half of its suburbs still rely on the pan system.

Furthermore, more than 400,000 Italians migrated to this country after the war. To my knowledge we have not brought to this country unknown germs or new pestilences.

Dear madam, apparently your travelling has not taught you one thing: that there is good and bad everywhere and that sometimes a bit of tolerance and understanding for other people's problems would make life more pleasant and improve relationship between human beings.

Comment. In 1974, the Aussie habit of slandering foreigners had reduced a little probably. We have relaxed our xenophobic myopia that greeted the huge influx of migrants from Europe for a decade after the War, and are accepting them more and more as decent people.

Our White Australia Policy was about to be removed, and that meant that a trickle, and then **a landslide, of Asians** would soon enough come to live and work with us. But with these, the **average** Aussie was reasonably well behaved, and did **not revive the worst of our old habit of thoroughly denigrating the newcomers.**

MARCH NEWS ITEMS

A small group of Aborigines took advantage of **the Queen's visits to Canberra. They booed and cat-called her**, and three of them went to a Government Office and confronted staff there with a pistol....

This was unusual behaviour for our Aborigines. In the past, they showed little sign of emulating US blacks who were in the forefront of violence and protest.,,,

Perhaps it was a sign of things to come? They were specifically **campaigning for land rights**.

By contrast, in Sydney, **Princess Anne and her husband, Mark Phillips, were cheered** by 1,500 school children massed to greet them. They spent the day hob-knobbing with dignitaries, and then went horse-riding.

Despite the Aboriginal protest, the brief visit of the Queen and family made it clear that the **vast majority of citizens still supported the Royal Family**.

A pop star, David Casey, was mobbed at his Sydney performance at Randwick Racecourse in Sydney. Sixty girls were reported as injured, and 200 others suffered heatstroke. This was **a decade** where overseas so-called **stars got rave audiences** for shouting from the stage.

US President, Richard Nixon, is still squirming. He has again confirmed that he is willing to co-operate with a Committee that is deciding whether he will face impeachment charges....

But he added so many conditions that there was no chance of getting his true position. Once again, **his grand beating of his chest convinced more of the American public of his guilt.**

A Japanese soldier has surrendered himself to Philippine authorities **after hiding in the jungle since 1945.** He believed for most of that time that Japan would never surrender, and that it was his duty to stay hidden until they returned to the islands.

Catholics the world over use their Rosary Beads to help them in their prayers. A typical string contains 50 beads, a few others, and a crucifix. **Many persons kiss the crucifix on completion of their prayers....**

Some doctors and scientists are saying that this latter habit **may be causing lead poisoning,** and the fondling of the beads may also be raising lead levels. Most beads are made of wood, so **a brief brush with the crucifix will not induce poisoning.**

The moral: do not put your crucifix into your mouth and suck it.

A survey of 200 households in suburbia asked what was the **most popular event of the weekend.** The winner was the Sunday barbie. Not far behind were Sunday lunch, watching sport, and Church....

Low on the list was night-clubbing, and the entertainment at beer gardens. Completely missing was the Saturday night Old Time Dance at the Community Hall.

YOUR DYING DUTY

In 1974, dying was a costly business. The seven States, the two Territories, and the Federal Government all saw to that. NSW was typical.

NSW residents were subject to **two forms of taxation. Firstly,** their estate consisted in the family home, plus everything they might have accumulated or saved. When a person died, their estate was hit with a bill for Death Duties. This was calculated as a percentage of the value of the estate. **Secondly**, the estate was charged with a Federal Tax, most often called an Estate Tax, about half the amount of value of the Death Duty.

These two taxes added together took a lot away from the beneficiaries. For example, **in NSW in 1949,** from an **estate worth 50,000 Pounds, the tax-men got 25,000 Pounds.** That is 50 per cent. And higher if the value of the estate was bigger.

By the 1970s, inflation was on the rapid rise, so that the values of estates were galloping and the taxes payable were galloping too.

Not surprisingly, agitation was also growing, and complaints were common. For example, see this Letter below.

Letters, A Dent. The Senate Standing Committee, after a two-year study, has reported on death duties and reached the obviously correct and gratifying conclusions that two death duties (State and Federal) are inconvenient, costly and unjust and the

Committee recommends that this dual system should be abolished. **Either** the Federal Government should take over the whole field (as it did with Income Tax in 1941) and make appropriate repayments to the States **or**, the Federal Government should withdraw and the six States pass uniform legislation to collect their own taxes.

Either course would require the co-operation of the Federal and State Governments and this, unfortunately, is difficult to envisage.

In its 75-page report, the Senate Committee in addition believed death duties inefficient and socially unacceptable. Furthermore, that the States should examine the possibilities of gradually reducing their death duties with a view to eventual abolition.

Maybe, therefore, at long last we can look forward to some relief from these iniquitous taxes within the foreseeable future, and most definitely this is one report that must not be allowed to be pigeonholed and forgotten.

By that date, opposition to the taxes had reached a crescendo. The argument against the taxes was that during a person's life, he works hard and accumulates assets. He is taxed on everything he earns. Then he dies, and after that he is taxed again. Hardly fair.

At the same time, all sorts of tax dodges had developed. For example, the person on his death bed could give away his fortune and end up with no assets. But Governments quickly stifled this rort by introducing a Gift Tax. A more beneficial rort was forming Companies that operated overseas, in a tax haven country, that had favourable taxation systems.

In any case, Governments in Australia thought it was time to remove what now was "an iniquitous tax". So from the mid-seventies, this was done. In the various States, at a range of times, some or all of them did remove both Death Duties and Estate Taxes.

Mind you, it took a few years to do the full job. And some vestiges still remain. But, by 2024, both taxes have substantially gone. **Rejoice. Rejoice.**

There is always a "But".... **But** the Government did not like losing so much money. Thus, about these years, it introduced, and then increased, a GST tax that more or less made up for death duties. It just hit different tax-payer at a different pace over more time.

But beware. There is a trap waiting, always ready to be sprung. There are many people who think that, when times are bad, the easiest way out for the nation is to **raise GST a few percentage points**.

So, **do rejoice. But keep your fingers crossed.**

THY WILL BE NOT DONE

In 1974, if a person died, and if he had a Will, and three children, he might have bequeathed that the estate be split into three equal parts. Such apportionments were common.

But suppose the person before death had an argument with one such child. The threat "I'll cut you out of my Will" was uttered and indeed, that new provision was entered into the Will.

Then, the offending child was disinherited. **Was that fair?** Maybe that child had spent a life dedicated to the parent, maybe had lived with him for decades, and had supported the parent through thick and thin. **Really, was that fair? Perhaps just because of a trivial spat?**

There are a million scenarios that are much the same, and they came to the fore in the free-thinking period of change that was the Whitlam period.

So, from about this time, the various States, and Territories, and the Commonwealth Government, started to change the laws around the execution of Wills. This was not just one grand moment of enlightenment. It was in fact a slow and tortuous process where every jurisdiction crawled sideways crab-like towards a better system.

So, **without intervening details**, let me jump ahead 50 years, to 2024. **The laws, controlling the distribution of assets, have changed.** We will focus on aspects that relate to **the challenging of the Will**s.

Now, in the year 2024, the aggrieved party in my above example, can challenge the Will. The party who was given no money at all can challenge the other two parties' share, and have an external mediator, or a Supreme Court judge, decide who gets what.

I am now going to do something brave. I will summarise 50 years of intense legislative activity, and legal activity, across nine jurisdictions, into just a few short sentences.

Here goes. In 1974, a person could expect that when he nominated certain people to get specific payouts from his Will, **his wishes would be granted**.

Now, after 50 years, **his wishes will not always be granted**, and the final decision on the payout in some cases will be made by a third party.

The example below is from a typical reported case. From an estate worth $2.4 million, with each of three children nominated to got $800,000, one child claimed that another should get only $100,000. That's a big difference.

Comment. I hasten to reassure most people who are not aware of the current situation, or who have not realised its pertinence. **Most people do not challenge.** It **does** cost a lot of money to make a challenge. Courts **are** often reluctant to change the payouts. Most people **do** accept the terms of the Will.

But some do not, and a fair percentage end in the Court system. **Often enough, the terms of the Will are not exercised.**

FOX HUNTING

Letters, B Weston. Re the article by Gavin Souter on the subject of flying foxes. It was surprising to learn that colonies exist in suburban gullies around Sydney.

One very large dormitory is located in "Fox Gully" near Jamberoo on the South Coast, and as a boy half a century ago I would see them flying past on their nightly forays on orchards from where we lived about six miles north of there.

They travelled at various heights according to where they were heading for, some within gunshot of the ground, and others would pass at considerable altitude across the face of the moon like witches on broomsticks.

On such nights the district would resound with the banging of shotguns as residents defended their fruit trees against the invaders. Taking up a firing position down-moon of several trees, advantage was taken of the giant bat's habit of doing a momentary hover before alighting and losing himself in the foliage.

In the late 1890s, the Governor of NSW, Viscount Hampden, was invited by my grandfather, Major E Weston of Albion Park, to join in a flying fox extermination shoot in Fox Gully.

With his entourage, he himself was equipped with three double-barreled shotguns and two menservants as loaders.

The party arrived mid-morning at Albion Park by special train, which then waited in the siding all day while they were all driven in buggies and gigs to the scene of action.

After a picnic lunch, they all descended to the floor of the ravine, from which thousands of foxes could be seen hanging asleep from the dense tree growth overhead. The first volley brought down dozens and put the rest in circling flight which created partial darkness below.

The Governor, perched on a rock, had a field day and his continuous firepower soon had him resembling King Harold at Hastings, the centre of a sea of bodies; **the day's bag** being estimated at upwards of two thousand.

It was a very weary and very smelly member of the aristocracy who finally boarded the train and headed for Sydney.

Comment. The end of my once-in-a-book period of indulgence.

I hope you too enjoyed it.

I have included the Letter above as a bit of fun. Now, at the end of March, **the industrial wheels are again fully turning** and the Letters and Headlines are getting more and more serious. So, as a bit of relief for both you and me, I have indulged myself with this bit of nonsense.

But, at the same time, I am asking myself, how readers will react to this wanton slaughter. When this was written, such conduct by humans was acceptable.   **How does the reader in the mid-twenties feel about it?**

DIFFERENT POINTS OF VIEW

Letters, (Mrs) G Baker. This week I travelled on a city-bound bus via Oxford Street to Martin Place. At Kingsford, a quite elderly couple sat in the front seat atop the double-decker. Even before the American accent was heard, one knew by the inevitable slung camera that they were tourists.

If ever I wanted a demonstration of how the ordinary working class Australian feels about America, it was made clear by the attitudes of practically every passenger. Those seated near, pointed to various buildings and advised the visitors on places worth seeing. As the advisers forsook their seats and others took them, the same thing happened, some even walking from the back to say: "Welcome, have a nice time."

As they and I alighted at Park Street, I showed them how to go across to St James Station. The lady had tears in her eyes and said she and her husband had been overwhelmed at finding such kindness and friendliness. Back home, their papers are telling them how much Australia dislikes them.

I wish I could send a letter like this to an American paper, letting them know our true feelings and apologising for the rudeness and ingratitude, voiced by some people, whose vocal chords are heard louder (apparently in the USA) than the fair-dinkum Aussies are here.

I felt very proud to be an Australian. Gestures like this, I feel, cement bonds and good neighbours more than all the back-slapping and policy speeches.

Before you get that nice warm glow from the above Letter, you better have a look at the one below.

Letters, H Greenwald. When I was a tourist here, people were nice to me too. After all I was going home soon and therefore was no threat to anybody. But since coming here to live, it's another story.

How much pride does Mrs Baker, or anyone else, take in the fact that her Government is making it impossible for me to get a job in my field. Because I am a broadcaster, I have been told repeatedly that "this is a bad time for people with foreign accents because Senator Doug McClelland is breathing down our necks to get more Australian content on the air."

One station executive told me: "We get calls whenever we've had an American working for us complaining that we should have given the job to an Australian."

I didn't migrate to this country to become an American, I came here to become an Australian, but it's obvious that this can never happen unless I start talking like one. At no time has anyone told me my qualifications to work in the broadcasting business here weren't good enough. One outfit went so far as to give me the ludicrous excuse that I was "over-qualified."

It seems that Senator McClelland has terrorised the broadcasting industry and for that reason I'm supposed to throw 16 years of experience down the drain because I talk like an American.

Next time Mrs Baker, and others, are so quick to pat themselves on the back for being nice to tourists, they might do well to remember those tourists are no threat to them. They haven't come here to live and take up a precious job. No, those tourists are going home and taking their accents with them, a situation which should make Senator McClelland sleep easier.

Comment. The truth often depends on where you are looking from.

APRIL NEWS ITEMS

In New York, in Times Square, **a ticker tape** has run continuous news headlines **since 1928**. Now the proprietor of the tape has decided that, **in future, the tape will carry only good news stories....**

He says that "**I am sick of headlines about war, kidnapping, and budget deficits.** I've had it with bad news."

A headline from the *Sydney Morning Herald* on April 2nd said PETROL TO FLOW AGAIN IN SYDNEY TODAY. The next day the headline was DRIVERS' STRIKE HALTS PETROL AGAIN....

This is typical of life in our major cities. A vast range of strikes, random or planned, brief or long-term, necessary or frivolous, all kept citizens on their toes. They affected all travel, postage, building of houses or units or giant towers. Some disruption of normal living was stirring everyone every week.

Last year the Canberra Art Gallery bought an abstract painting known as *Blue Poles*, painted by Jackson Pollock. **This was a very controversial purchase**, with criticism directed at the "waste of public money." Many also claimed that the painting was "scarcely worthy of showing in any art gallery...."

It has **now arrived in Sydney** on loan from Canberra, for two months. Lots of security guards, police, secrecy, and air conditioning to keep it at a uniform temperature. On a huge 17 foot by 8 foot canvas, it will be covered with preserving wax to maintain its colours....

When publicly displayed, it is expected to draw record viewers. **Not all of them will have forgotten their opposition to the purchase.**

Remember the heiress Patricia Hurst who was reportedly kidnapped? She is back in the news with a letter, and a spoken tape to a newspaper stating she is well, not under any compulsion, and free and active. She was not kidnapped, she left to join the Symbionese Liberation Army, and is critical of all aspects of American capitalism. She is critical of her father as a magnate furthering the capitalist cause....

She sent photographs of herself holding a gun in front of a Symbionese Army flag....

Authorities are wondering whether this letter was forced from her. But later developments showed she was genuine. We will come back to this intriguing story as it develops....

The Symbionese Liberation Army was a far-left anti-capitalist group with the familiar calls to militant action. Apart from the Patty Hurst kidnapping, they were guilty of one murder, and several bank robberies at gun-point, and a multitude of plans to overthrow the vile system they were thriving under....

They came to a sticky end (see later) and survived as an organisation only from 1973 to 1975.

WHITLAM GOES TO THE POLLS

Early in April, the Labor Federal Government announced that the new Ambassador to Ireland would be a man called Vincent Gair. Mr Gair had been an ex-Labor Senator and was nearly retired from active politics.

The Liberal Opposition did not like this. "Jobs for the boys." It was in the position that **it** held control of the Senate, while Labor controlled the House of Representatives.

So, the Liberal Leader, Billy Snedden, threatened that if Gair was not blocked from taking the position, then the Liberal Party would use its Senate majority to "block supply." **This meant that it would cut off all money that the Government needed to run its business.** This in turn would mean that all seats in Parliament would be vacated, both the Senate and the House, and fresh elections would be called.

This double dissolution was a big deal. It meant that if the Liberals were fully successful, they would have unchecked power to do what they liked. If Labor was fully successful, **it** would have that power.

There had been only two occasions in the past where such a double dissolution had happened. **It was a winner -take-all ploy.**

By April 12, Whitlam accepted Snedden's ultimatum and, after visiting the Governor General for permission, announced that an election **would be held in just over a month**.

The political scene in the next few months will be very active.

As a side issue, consider the Senators who had been newly elected about 15 months prior. They doubtless rejoiced because they felt secure in their position for the next six years. **Now**, they were back on the election trail, stumping round, drumming up support. **Ouch.**

Comment. Leaving aside the political inferences from the upcoming election, I think it would be good for the nation if **one Party or the other won both Houses.** For 16 months now, much legislation had been smothered in Parliament by each of two Parties having the power to block initiatives. It would be nice to see all **the executive control in the hands of a single Party**, and thus remove constraints on the implementation of welcome reforms.

MORAL POLLUTION

A public rally by **conservative groups** on a Sunday in Sydney's Hyde Park drew a crowd of 25,000, a third of which were teenagers. They carried banners which read "fight truth decay", "pornography stinks", "moral pollution needs a solution".

The Anglican Dean of Sydney summed up the mood of the rally.

News Item. Mr Shilton said: "The fair dinkum Aussie is beginning to see for himself that he is being got at by the miserably manipulators in this country.

"For too long they have been trying to white ant our society with their fallacious philosophies and their sleazy propaganda.

"The manipulators have masqueraded under the catchcry of freedom. By claiming a free go for themselves they have hoodwinked unsuspecting people into giving a free go to the Devil."

He called upon voters to demand that the nation's political leaders declare, before the election, their views on issues such as pornography, divorce, euthanasia and abortion.

"I believe there are sufficient people in Australia today who are so deeply concerned about these moral issues that the margin of swing either way could be influenced by the answers given. You give Christ a go when you stand up and be counted."

News Item. Dr Clair Isbister, of the Royal North Shore Hospital, was loudly cheered for her speech.

She said Australian mothers did not want easier divorce, abortion on demand, homosexual aberrations treated as normal behaviour, contraceptive vending machines in schools, and sex education from the television program, No. 96.

"Our laws forbid cockroaches in restaurant kitchens and cats served in the stew, but they do not seem to protect us from violence and pornography," she said.

"We are not concerned with minor matters such as streaking - about people who wish to display their deficiencies in public - but about major issues of real concern.

"We accept seat belts because they save lives. By what right can Senator Murphy (the Federal Attorney-General) over-rule accepted behaviour without our consent? We are the community and it is we who determine community standards.'
Comment. This rally must have been very good news for the organisers of this Festival of Light campaign. It attracted a big crowd, and was truly ecumenical in that it brought out all sorts of Protestant clergymen, as well as the top Catholic hierarchy. Such public demonstrations of religious faith and morality were rare at this time and, no doubt, this result was most gratifying to the organisers.

BIRTHDAY CARD PROBLEMS

Letters, B Sewell. I have just spent my lunch hour trying to purchase a humorous birthday card to give to my sister. I gave up.

The only cards I could find can only be described as filth. I am not a prude. I am reasonably broad-minded, but I was shocked with the cards which were so predominantly displayed.

The shops I tried were not in the back streets, and they included a branch of a store bearing the name of prominent Sydney family.

If a market does exist for this type of card, and I have no doubt one does, I plead with the stores not to presume we all want them and so not to give them so much prominence in the displays.

The irony is they are next to or opposite Easter cards in some stores.

Letters,   (Mrs)   M   Wellington. While sympathising with Mr Sewell and his inability to find a suitable card for his sister, please spare a thought for the "get well" card buyers. All the humorous "get well" cards assume the patient is a sex maniac or has a lavatorial sense of humour. It's almost impossible to find an appropriate card with an optimistic message for a seriously ill patient, male or female.

Comment. Moral corruption has apparently spread to the greeting card industry.

EFFECTS OF STRIKES

The ongoing strike epidemic obviously affected all persons in many obvious ways, but some ways are not so obvious. Take for example, the following Letter.

Letters, D de Keizer. Following recent postal strikes, I am writing to make an appeal to the Postal Workers' Union to handle mail from the correspondence school during mail strikes.

I am a third-form student attending the Nepean District School for Crippled Children. All secondary students at this school are enrolled at the correspondence school and, owing to recent postal strikes, routine has been completely disrupted and many of us have been without lessons for periods of up to a fortnight.

Being physically disabled, we find it difficult enough to return the required amount of work without interruptions to our routine caused by postal strikes.

If we are to take our places vocationally in society (this being our aim and surely our right) we must achieve high academic qualifications. We feel that frequent postal strikes will place our future in jeopardy.

I have written this letter in the hope that people may become aware of our plight.

GOOD NEWS FOR PARENTS

The Federal election next month is starting to produce the promises from politicians. One such is that the Government will introduce a new scheme that will provide after-school care for young children, as well as pre-school care for toddlers.

The reader in the 1920's will remember the details, and the changes, and the ups-and-downs of the programme over the last 50 years. But back in 1974, this was a brave new initiative, and a great vote-catcher.

As a side issue, it reinvigorated the argument of whether mothers who went to work were robbing their children of the support they needed in their early years. Some mothers said it did, and others said it did not.

I have no intention of reviving that argument here, but I should record that by the 2020's it has mainly gone away. Most young parents in their twenties and thirties just take it for granted that Mum will go back to work in a few months, and they budget their mortgage with that expectation.

Comment. The child-care field has grown to the stage where it is an industry in its own right. Governments shake in their boots if it suggests that it might strike for some cause. What was initially a smattering of relatives and girls who could not get a job, has grown into a certificated, professional, group with organised career paths.

Second comment. As someone said once "Out of the humble acorn do mighty oaks grow."

PATRICIA HURST

Patricia is back in the news. She is no longer seen as the innocent victim of a kidnapping, and has changed to an active supporter of the Symbionese Liberation Army, This is confirmed by an unchallenged video tape of the Army **robbing a bank in San Francisco** with Miss Hurst clearly shown. She appears as an active participant, **brandishing a sawn-off shotgun**, and full of life.

Comment. You should note that this "Army" was not one really. In fact it was just a student-type group that was set up by a dozen left-wingers to destroy capitalism. It seems to have had 50 followers on a good day, and existed for less that 10 years. It stood out for a while because it was prepared to back up its extremist words with concrete violence.

ANOTHER DEMAND FOR MONEY

Police responded to calls from a male voice that threatened to blow up a Qantas flight in mid air. The caller demanded $500,000 to cancel the explosion. After a series of calls and demands, and discussions of how the ransom was to be delivered and paid, the police raided a suburban house in Sydney's South Granville with all the drama of massed policemen and high-powered rifles.

In the house, they found a 15-year-old boy and arrested him. He had no accomplices, and no idea of how he would execute the threat. He was charged with two counts of demanding money with menaces.

Comment. Such real threats were, at the moment, very popular, both here and abroad.

POSTAL STRIKES

Probably the most annoying of the regular strikes afflicting the nation were those affecting transport, and petrol. These affected the movements of people, getting to work and school and sport. And they affected deliveries of goods and services. They had the nation very cross.

But almost as bad were the recurrent postal strikes. These could just be at mail-sorting facilities, or refusal to deliver, or work-to-regulations frustrations at the counter. Or just walk-off-the job for short or long terms.

So millions of mail articles were not being delivered, or being delivered weeks late. Mail was piling up at

Post Offices. Some mail was not being collected from overloaded red Post Office boxes. In fact, a complete and efficient stuff-up.

Letters,   R   Carruthers. Who   does   the Postmaster-General, Mr Bowen, think he is fooling by giving the impression that Sydney's major mail dispute has been settled?

While the Redfern and Artarmon exchanges may be operating more smoothly, they are just a drop in the bucket compared with the chaos at suburban post-offices where mail is still being delayed.

Union action often means that delivery runs can't be completed within the time of the restricted working hours, and it's not always known if what mail does get through will be delivered from one day to the next. As a subscriber to a number of Australian and overseas periodicals, I am furious about not having received any second-class mail for more than a month.

After making inquiries to the Federal Executive of the Amalgamated Postal Workers' Union, in Melbourne, I was informed that the New South Wales branch had been instructed to lift the work-bans before negotiations on its claims could proceed. However, the instructions are being ignored.

How can Mr Bowen or the Unions expect support for the Labor Government at next month's election?

Letters, I Nankervis. This morning I again waited with bated breath for the sound of the postie's whistle in the expectation of receiving a cheque to help my ailing business and placate my patient bank manager.

But no - again only one letter and that was a bill! This makes a total of six letters this month and all of them bills.

However, I took heart when I read this morning that at last the Postmaster-General had taken some interest and successfully appealed to the postal workers to lift their ban on the 3,000 bags of mail wherein I hope some cheques for me may lie.

The grounds for the PMG's appeal were that **the bans could affect Labor's election chances!** It appears, therefore, that we can all take heart and know that between now and May 18, the mails will go through and perhaps other strikers and creators of industrial unrest will respond to similar appeals - **until the elections are over.**

After May 18, what then? If Labor is returned the answer is obvious and there I rest my case.

Comment. These are just two of a multitude of such complaints. Both of them refer to the looming Federal election, and suggest that maybe this will somehow provide solutions.

Hopeful, they **may** be. But **disappointed**, they certainly **will** be.

TAXI PLATES

In Taxi talk, a "plate" refers to the licence that an operator needs before he can run a taxi service. The licence must come from a Government Department, and comes with a number of performance standards that the operator must meet.

The number of licences issued is restricted, and since they can be passed from person to person, they become a form of currency. If you have one, you can sell it for a sum of money. The restrictions are such that a Sydney plate costs about $25,000 or more.

At the same time, taxis are hard to get at many times. The Letter below talks a little about this.

Letters, P Royle. In the Great Taxi Problem, or should one say scandal, I am one of the people who have to depend on taxis for transport. Except for off-periods in the daytime, it is nearly impossible to get one.

I have spoken to many drivers and argued that there should be more available. The reply is, generally, that there are plenty of cabs idle because there are no drivers: the wages are not good enough.

The next thing will be an application for higher rates so that additional expenses can be met.

The solution to this shortage would be to issue another 2,000 plates to persons of good reputation who have had experience in the industry. This would bring out the drivers who are not finding it worthwhile to drive today.

There is something wrong when, in spite of a lack of drivers, people are prepared to pay up to $28,000 for a plate.

Visitors to Sydney from overseas find the securing of taxi transport impossible. I have travelled all over the world, and anywhere else there is no problem.

Someone should realise that there must be a powerful body keeping the Department of Motor Transport from issuing more plates.

Why should a plate be worth $28,000 if business is so bad?

Comment. This Letter just scratches the surface. The situation in Sydney, and most other cities, is indeed scandalous. Clearly illicit money is changing hands, and clearly some politicians are not as vigilant as they should be in scrutinising this industry.

MAY NEWS ITEMS

Sir Frank Packer died in Sydney's Prince Albert Hospital. He had been Chairman of *Consolidated Press Holdings* and Publisher of the *Daily Telegraph* and *Sunday Telegraph*. **He funded two challenges for yachting's America's Cup.**

Attempts to **mould the three major Protestant congregations into a single uniform body** met with mixed success, though with some dissent from minor factions in the Congregationalist and Methodist Churches....

The Presbyterians also agreed, but with **527 of their 1437 ministries deciding to stay with the Old Church.**

The Communist Party in Australia had reached its hey day about 1950. But a Liberal Party election advertisement for **commercial TV** stirred up some ghosts....

It said that "**Labor is disguised Communism.**" Labor said that this was not true, and that **anti-Communist feelings would be revived by running it on TV, all to the detriment of Labor. It is now before the Courts....**

Here we are 25 years after Reds were under all Beds in 1949, and the **bogey of Communism still loiters.**

All major city newspapers in Sydney were on strike yesterday for the weekend. The strikers demands included a sixth week of annual leave over their existing five. Executive staff are able to do the printers' job so as to produce very limited editions. ...

But if you look for comics on Sunday, or an account of the ballet, too bad.

Fifty-five per cent of people surveyed in the US thought that **Nixon should resign or be impeached.** This compares with 30 per cent last August.

A **Post Office van was forced off** the road forty miles north of Brisbane. The contents of the van were then stolen. This was a sum of money, of value about $500,000, sent regularly from banks to banks. This is **the second biggest heist in Australia's history.**

The Federal Government conducted a poll of 60,000 people to decide **what our National Anthem should be.** **52 per cent voted for** *Advance Australia Fair.* 20 per cent voted for *Waltzing Matilda.* All of these are suggestions. They are not official and cannot be enforced. *God Save the Queen* should be played only when the Queen is present....

Keep in mind that when the Liberals get back into power, they will probably change the National Anthem back to *God Save the Queen* again.

In a last-minute attempt to sway voters, Opposition Leader Bill Snedden said that **his** plan would see pensions rise faster than under Labor. **Labor counter-claimed.** What a pity to see policy-poor Parties in such obvious ploys.

RAILROADED BY OFFICIALDOM

Letters, (Miss) F Ross. On February 26, I was involved in an accident when my vehicle was forced off the road at the Eungai rail bridge, down an embankment and almost on to the railway line.

I was taken by ambulance, and admitted to Macksville Hospital. On returning home on April 15, I found a letter from the District Superintendent of Railways stating that I had caused the rail line to be closed, delaying a goods train for 31 minutes.

Because of the delay, Public Transport Commission **costs amounting to $9** had been incurred and prompt payment of this account was requested.

Why does the Public Transport Commission not charge striking guards etc at the rate of $9 for each 31-minute delay caused to the running of the trains and for gross inconvenience to the general public?

Am I to be penalised for something that was beyond my control? I consider this imposition of $9 an insult and a victimisation of a member of the general public.

Comment. What can I say?

EVEN THE ABC

Radio and TV programs from the ABC were closed down for most of the day when ABC technicians walked off the job. And they plan to hold a 24-hour stoppage starting noon Saturday.

That will affect all sports broadcasts and Saturday night viewing.

Comment. Even the mighty ABC is vulnerable to strikes.

COMMENT ON ELECTION

The Federal election is just three weeks away. This election was called without much notice, and caught all our parliamentarians on the hop. So that probably explains why the normal numbers of their promises are so few.

Granted, there was Whitlam's offer of child-care relief for the masses. That was a big one. But after that, just the usual vague suggestion that one or other Party would raise wages, or perhaps cut wages. Some Party would hold an inquiry into something or other, or there might be a scheme announced to counter inflation. Nothing out of the ordinary, and voters remained not at all excited or agitated. Still, who knows, with three weeks to go, perhaps maybe someone will liven things up.

ELECTION LETTERS

Letters to Editors abounded. I have picked out a few, **not** because they attempted to present **the accepted case** for a particular Party. But **because they did not do that**, and give perhaps a view of something different.

Letters, (Mrs) J Simpson. I am astounded and deeply angered by the type of election material being presented to the public on television.

In particular I refer to the migrant woman speaking of **her family's escape from tyranny** in her own country to find a similar situation in Australia under the present Government.

I object strongly to the implications in such disturbing and false propaganda.

Letters, D Regan. The main issue in the coming elections is not inflation, important as that is, but freedom. The Labor Party has introduced some needed reforms but, in the long run, it stands for socialism, with the possible threat of a Communist takeover. Inflation, which it has done nothing to control, increases this risk.

The Liberal-Country Party has its faults, but it promises reasonable inflationary curbs and a gradual reform program on democratic lines to benefit all Australians. It was in fact a Liberal government which pioneered much of what Labor promises, eg. Federal aid for education. Give Snedden and Anthony a fair go!

Letters, P Graham. Reflection in Anzac Week reminded us of all the debts we owe for the sacrifices of others. Reflection in election week will remind us of all the sacrifices we have made for the debts of others.

Nothing is more certain than that the Federal Labor Government has overspent. And we the Australian public have had to pay the price, our income tax contributions having gone up by over 25 per cent in the space of less than a year.

Let's not forget that the overspending has been founded on the "I'm all right Jack" principle. Never before have we seen such a lack of altruism than has been reflected in the Labor regime. On May 18 remember all the champagne flights around the world, all the jobs for the boys (not to mention Mum and the kids) and all the empire building.

Mr Snedden's promise to return $600 million a year to the real workers by reducing income tax is more like what this country needs.

Letters, E Faulder. As an insurance agent with a major life office (Australian-based) with nine years' experience, I should like to thank the Prime Minister.

Mr Whitlam has always been outspoken, knowing and mighty in his directing the people of this nation. To the Victorian farmers... "You never had it so good." To the residents of Galston.... "You're getting Galston."

And it is on this basis that I should like to convey my thanks to him for his assistance and encouragement to the life insurance industry, particularly its representatives, who, without new business sales, don't eat.

You don't know, Mr Whitlam, how important life insurance proceeds are to widows and their children. People still die. And you don't know how important insurance savings are to a man and a woman as they approach retirement. People still grow old.

People who buy life insurance, I believe, have qualities of concern for others, common sense and vision. They are the kind of people with the capacity to do things for themselves and to think for themselves. Not your kind of people, Mr Whitlam? I believe those characteristics apply to a lot of people in this country.

Your Treasurer, Mr Crean, has heavily increased taxation on all life companies through the last Budget, **lowering** interest returns to policy holders, and **casting sufficient doubt** on the continuance of the $1,200 allowable tax deduction for life insurance savings, making it hard for all parties - buyer, agent and company - to know "just where we are at" and "just what you're up to."

You are costing people much of their planned savings, Mr Whitlam. Including this family. I now work from morning to midnight to earn a much reduced living. Thanks. For nothing.

Letters, C Clague. Mr Askin's Estonian-born, Australian-citizen, lady friend would be a lot less starry-eyed about her Liberal-Country Party friends if she had dared venture outside her comfortable middle-class urban existence to view what life was like for an equivalent ethnic minority group under Liberal-Country Party Australian Government.

Who would deny her statements that Estonians, and indeed the members of a number of ethnic minority groups in the Soviet Union, have suffered and indeed still suffer much, that their freedom is restricted, and that fundamental human and citizen rights have been denied them.

Aboriginal Australians stand in proportion to the total Australian population much as do Estonians to the total population of the States of the Soviet Union. Rates of Aboriginal infant mortality and morbidity through the 1960s and beyond, depressed housing, denial of their rights to their own lands, denial of any voice in their own affairs, denial of award wages and social security benefits sum up the evidence of the repressive, racist policies of Liberal-Country Party governments towards Australia's indigenous ethnic minority.

Aboriginal Australians in the Northern Territory in particular are only now, under Labor, beginning to breathe the air of freedom and social justice which "Mrs Estonian" applauds as fundamentally Australian since she has enjoyed it here as a member of a "favoured class" and which she was denied as a member of an equivalent oppressed ethnic minority in the Soviet Union.

If she is sincere in her condemnation of governments which oppress minority communities, then she has offered the most tangible argument of the election campaign so far for voting Labor.

ELECTION BUILD-UP

When Whitlam decided that he would force a double dissolution onto Parliament, he would have been very confident that he could come back from the election with **control of both Houses**. After all, at the time, he already had control of the Lower House, and sadly needed the same control over an annoying Senate.

What he hoped for was that his fifteen months as Prime Minister, and his very generous treatment of large parts of the workforce, would sway voters in his favour. As well that his social change agenda had been generally acknowledged as welcome. On the other hand, the Liberal Opposition was just drifting along, and had yet to find a forceful voice, or decent policies, to support it.

This type of logic was comforting to his supporters. Yet, as the election grew close, a number of decent polls kept saying the result **for** Labor was not assured,.

GROUP THERAPY

Throughout the last few days of the election campaign, there have been a large number of Letters from **groups** that want to **tell other voters how to vote**. They have been doctors from Canberra, and an equal number from the country urging the dead opposite. Groups of physiotherapists, of farmers, of teachers, "85 influential clergymen and women", all arguing and pleading for votes for their preferred Parties.

The writer below takes an overview position on this, and using **the clergy as his specific target**, talks about why all **such groups are worthy of acceptance** only with adequate care.

Letters, R James. I read with amazed and amused disgust statements that 85 influential churchmen and women had signed a document urging all Christians to vote Labor on May 18.

The list of signatories makes interesting reading - Anglicans, Methodists, Church of Christ and so on.

When one considers the infighting that takes place in churches represented by these people, the immaturity, insecurity and false ideology of these signatories are all the more evident.

The Anglicans cannot decide whether they are high or low churchmen. They still argue loudly and at length as to whether they or the Roman Catholic people have an unbroken line from St Peter's Church. They fight intensely on forms of worship as to whether one should genuflect, make the sign of the cross and attend confession.

The Methodists, Congregationalists and Presbyterians have been trying for years to form a united church, and with little success. It would appear that the Presbyterian Church will probably, in the near future, have litigation over the dividing up of $200 million of assets. The Methodist Church is a large commercial property owner in all the capital cities and theologically is steeped in antiquity.

The Church of Christ prides itself on its broadmindedness, but states that Baptism by immersion is necessary for salvation, and this is denied by many other non-conformist churches.

Theologically, procedurally and in Christian charity, **the churches these people represent are poles apart, and each views the other with grave religious distrust**.

Can they, therefore, in real sincerity **expect any sane person to be influenced by isolated members of such split groups?**

THE ELECTION RESULT

The first reaction of commentators to the result was one of surprise. The Government had not won a landslide, nor had it won a narrow victory. In fact, the question, for the day after, was whether it had won at all.

As matters cleared over the next few days, it became clear that **Labor had indeed won in the House of Representatives**. But only by a majority of a seat or two. This meant a loss of about four seats.

Ouch, said Gough Whitlam. Ouch, said a swathe of arrogant Ministers who assumed that they were guaranteed a seat. Ouch, said the Labor Party apparatus who had expected to get control of both Houses with a comfortable majority.

But still, Labor did win, it appeared to have a working majority. But, wait a minute. That was only in the House. **What about the Senate?** Results from the Senate are always slow, and take a few days to settle down. What did they show? They showed that it was the tightest possible race, that both parties had an equal chance of gaining power and then by the slimmest majority of one Seat. And it took a month to reach to that conclusion.

SO, WHO WON?

Labor had enough seats to continue in government. But with a reduced majority in the House, and **a dubious majority in the Senate**, it was in a worse **numerical** position than it had been prior to the election.

Beyond that, the Labor machine suffered a loss in confidence. **Prior to the election,** Whitlam et al had an aura about them that said they were invincible, that their cause was on the up and up, and would soon reach complete triumph. **After the election**, this was clearly not the case. It was still arguable, but not everyone gave it as much credence as before.

MEANWHILE IN THE USA....

While the Australian election was finishing up, the Symbionese Liberation Army was in trouble at home. A quick raid on a grocery store in downtown LA, during which Patricia fired a shot, turned into a big police operation. Most of the would-be robbers fled to the gang-headquarters in the suburbs, and neighbours reported several heavily-armed girls were visible.

A force of over 400 police officers was assembled. These were backed up by personnel from the FBI, the Sheriffs Department, the State Highway Patrol, and the Fire Department. Over the next few hours, a siege ensued, in which over 9,000 rounds of ammunition were fired.

The headquarters were destroyed by fire, together with two adjoining properties. **Six Army leaders were killed. The entire action was shown live on TV for hours.** Hearst watched it all from a hotel room in Anaheim.

She went on to star again at later dates.

A word of advice. Unless you are **deadly** serious, be careful about the protest groups you get mixed up with.

THE ROLE OF WHEEL-TAPPERS

Have you ever sat in a steam-driven train and looked at the man who wanders along the tracks and stops regularly to tap the wheels. He always seems to be satisfied and just goes on the next wheel. Does he actually achieve anything? Or is this just an old ritual, now used to keep the person in a job?

The Letter below explains it all.

Letters, B Blanchard. In reply to A McElwain, and his attempt to rubbish the railway employee who taps the wheels of trains, may

I enlighten him on some aspects associated with these duties.

The "wheel tapper" is classified as a train-examiner whose duties entail checking of all wheels, braking systems, renewal of brake shoes and couplings before he issues a certificate to the driver that a goods or passenger train is in order before departure.

These duties are carried out in all weathers and poor lighting, with stock in trucks urinating over this chap. In addition, as railway records will prove, employees engaged as examiners have suffered amputations, in many cases fatal injuries.

Yes, Mr McElwain, your safety as a passenger depends on men such as "wheel tappers" and I think they deserve better recognition than your snide remarks in an endeavour to be humorous.

JUNE NEWS ITEMS

The Share Market crashed. Only seven, out of the 1,000 stocks traded, ended in the black. BHP fell 50 cents to $6.50. (In June 2024, it is $45.00).

Now that the election is over, the Government can reveal its plans. They include **a big tax increase for middle income earners....**

This increase is to help curb the rising rate of **inflation, currently at 13.6 per cent per annum.** This latter figure, from the Treasurer, comes as a bit of a shock. Prior to the election, **he said it was 8.6 per cent.**

The Anglican Bishop of Newcastle thinks it is appropriate if Anglicans **go to Sunday Church in their sports clothes.** There should be no need to change into Sunday best clothes if they are coming or going to leisure activities outside the Church.

The figures for inflation keep getting worse and worse. In mid-June, the prices of Peugeot, Chrysler, and Renault cars were raised **by eight percent.** The price of public hospital care **was raised by 50 per cent.....**

YES, I did say 50 per cent. In a public ward, the price will rise from $15 to $22.50 per day....

Everywhere, all of a sudden, **inflation** was on the lips as **Public Enemy Number One.**

The parents of 17 Australian Thalidomide **victims** will share a payment of $1.7 million from the Distillers

Company. The payment is **compensation for damages** caused to unborn babies by mothers using the drug during pregnancy....

Legal proceedings have persisted for eight years. The company will make offers to 25 other children after some medical questions have been answered.

An Irish terrorist died in a top-security English gaol at Parkhurst. He had been on a **hunger strike for two months** refusing all medical aid. He had been found guilty of planting car bombs in 1971 in London....

Two other women prisoners are on the point of dying at Brixton after vowing a hunger strike unless they were **transferred to an Irish gaol.** They, too, were sentenced to life for car bombing in London....

After 200 days, forced feeding has now been abandoned, and **they are on the point of death**....

Should prisoners be allowed to select their own place of incarceration? This is **the principle** being argued in Britain at the moment.

Post Office workers in NSW are continuing to strike or not strike as they please. Next week the Officers will return to work. But only for **one day in the next nine**. That means the total closure of most Branches for the nine days....

Trade Unions are demanding **a flat increase of $30 per week, plus** an "industrial allowance" of $4.50 per week. They want their normal **weekly shift was reduced** by four hours per week.

TIDYING UP THE ELECTION

Letters, B Weston. Now that all the ballyhoo of the election is over, it is interesting to note the debris.

Every second wall, shop-front, billboard, fence, awning, light-post - in fact, any place you look - is defaced with Labor Party or Communist Party posters.

Fair go, Gough - how about cleaning up your mess now you have won?

HOW SAFE ARE WE?

The next two Letters make a good point.

In 1974, the Vietnam War had gone away. This nation was behaving as if it was time to play. Was it?

Letters, M Tranter. Ten years ago, we were at the beginning of a small war in Vietnam. Then the drums rolled, the guns fired, and our young men were sent to the slaughter in a land they had never heard of. We spent almost a decade asking why we were fighting, what we were gaining, who we were killing in the jungles.

Now, two years after we stopped that folly, most of us have ceased asking those questions, and are right back at the stage of living and thinking as if it can never happen again. **Look at our headlines.** The trouble spots in the world are all round us. But they get no mention in our daily Press.

Look at your Letters column. Scarcely a mention of a potential   sauce of conflict for Australia. We are safe **again**, we are too far away **again**, we would not get dragged in **again**.

But, I urge you, **think again**. In 1964, no one thought we would be in a major conflict within two years. If it could happen then, can it not happen now?

Letters, I Armitage. Of all the dangerously irresponsible acts perpetrated against the people of Australia by the Whitlam Government, surely the downgrading of the Armed Forces is the most damaging and frightening.

I could hardly believe my ears on hearing for the first time the fatuous statement that "there could be no threat to Australia in the next 15 years."

Did anyone predict Hitler 15 years or even five years before his time, or Pearl Harbour, or the Japanese attack on Australia? Has the present Government clairvoyant powers denied to the rest of us?

With the news that India has carried out a nuclear test, and the facts reported by the Rt Rev Ian Shevill in his recent article "The Revival of Shinto there seems little doubt that before very long Japan must also have its nuclear capability, if it hasn't already got it. No threat to Australia? Japan with her thrusting millions; Australia with her vast open spaces and reserves of raw materials?

Finally Dennis Warner's article "Army without a Cause" gives the appallingly high rate of resignations of senior officers as well as other ranks since the Labor Government came to power; and sadder still the effect of Labor policy on the morale of those who remain.

Isn't there anyone in the Labor Government who has any understanding of these things? Isn't there anyone with a voice loud enough to cry in the wilderness. "Advance Australia Where?" should be Labor's next electioneering slogan - it fits!

Comment. Eternal vigilance? Sounds wise.

It comes with a benefit. The benefit of peace within. Does that mean that we all must be vigilant **all** the time? That is a heavy price.

Wiser heads than mine can decide this. I can't.

COUNTRY PUBLIC TRANSPORT

I have now written 36 of this Series of books. Every five years or so, I have a look at public transport to see if it is getting any closer to the Twentieth Century.

So, now in 1974, I will have another look.

Letters, (Mrs) M J Moxham. On May 2 I travelled to Nyngan on the Western Mail train, first class. I occupied a sleeping berth.

It was a cold night: the bunk was made up with only one thin blanket; always in the past two thick blankets have been supplied.

It became so cold I had to get up and get fully dressed to try to keep warm. The woman sharing the cabin with me had to do the same. We had to share one drinking glass.

At dawn we were brought a lukewarm cup of tea, without the water having boiled, by a junior attendant.

When I transferred to a diesel train at Dubbo, the carriages were bitterly cold, with no heating whatsoever. Two railway officials joined the train later, and they tried to light the gas heaters, but found all the gas cylinders were empty. There was no toilet paper in the lavatories.

I left the train at Nyngan, but many other unfortunate travellers had to endure these freezing conditions to Cobar.

My fare was only $5 less than the comfort of an airliner. Train travellers were offered more comfort on the Western Mail 50 years ago. Now services are being cut out because they are being poorly patronised, so the excuse goes.

But how can they be patronised when passengers are expected to endure what I and every other passenger suffered?

The Airways were no better.

Letters, (Miss) G Fortuin. Suffering the rigours of a journey by train from Melbourne, we decided to give ourselves comfortable clean travel on the return, and so booked by one of our premier much-advertised airlines.

Arriving at Mascot, our spirits were daunted by the sad and needlessly desolate no-man's-land appearance of the departure lounge - so, seeking to cheer ourselves, we went to the coffee-bar where all was quite grisly, notably the carpet all crumby and marked with months-long spots of sinister darkness.

Not anywhere in much travelling has neglect and dirt such as this been seen.

Less expenditure on advertising and more on basic necessities of hygiene might strengthen the image.

Letters, M Caiger. Is it possible for the Public Transport Commission to supply sleeping and buffet cars on the North Shore suburban rail system? This would greatly assist those of us who regularly spend hours waiting in the vain hope of reaching our destinations.

Perhaps also when entraining, the English-speaking platform personnel (if any) could advise an approximate ETA (to the nearest day would do).

To assist with alleviating the monotony, may I suggest that we be given pamphlets on such subjects as plant life, scenic views and speleology (for tunnel dwellers), so that we can thoroughly enjoy the surroundings during protracted delays.

I appreciate that the printing of these pamphlets might take a while, so in the interim perhaps the Commission could convert its Brunel and Stephenson class rolling stock from candle-power to electricity so that we may peruse this literature when made available.

Comment. The result from this small sample is pretty clear. Looks like the Twentieth Century will have to wait a few more years.

OUR RAILWAYS HAVE NO MONOPOLY

Last month I pointed out that most people were really cranky with our Public Transport and their facilities. From Letters received it was obvious that officials had no idea of how to meet the needs of their customers or of the idea of pleasing them.

But this attitude seems to be well entrenched in many parts of our daily lives, Whatever happened to the idea of "the customer is always right"? What happened to doctors making home visits? Can you find any grocers who will home deliver? Even to the sickest of customers?

Even our clergymen rarely visit newcomers to lay out the welcome mat.

All of this is inevitable, in our cities especially. As we grow up, business needs more rules and a less personal approach in order to prosper. And there will always be laggards who remain determinedly behind the times in service.

Some industries remain year after year resistant to improvement. Take the public transport system as one example. **As another**, take the industry that supplies amenities at public occasions, such as Country Shows, race meetings, football matches. Conditions there, including hygiene, are always bad.

Letters, R Wallis. After the Rugby match at the Cricket Ground last Saturday, there was no member of the Police Force to direct traffic at the South Dowling Street exit of one of the parking areas.

There were a lot of police at the ground, so surely one or more could have been detailed to this particular exit?

It's all right for the City Council to charge 40c for the privilege of parking there, but someone should have made arrangements to get the cars out. Some cars took almost one hour to get into South Dowling street.

But all was not lost, as eventually five young men organised themselves into a group to get the cars moving. To these unknown heroes, a word of thanks for a mighty job well done. There's hope for us yet.

Letters, R Jones. I write to you as one of the unfortunate spectators conned by the

Australian Rugby Union and the Sydney Cricket Ground Trust last Saturday.

Your sports writers have amply covered the disgraceful exhibition itself, but my gripe is directed at the appalling conditions and facilities foisted on the spectators.

For $2.50, I was admitted to the "Stand" area, and that was what I did: I stood - for 2 hours and 35 minutes, shoulder to shoulder amid empty beer cans, squashed pies and plastic cups on a hard concrete surface.

Occasionally I obtained glimpses of the dreary spectacle, between the heads and shoulders of other unfortunate exploited victims. The parking facilities are adequate, but getting in and out of them can be believed only if experienced.

In all, timing my trip, by car, to and from Darlinghust, and including my time in the SCG pigsty, I bombed 5 1/2 hours of my life. For this privilege I paid $2.90 to the ARU and the SCG Trust and $1.25 in wasted petrol - a total of $4.15.

It would have cost more had I been foolish enough to eat or drink any of the dangerous-looking concoctions on sale - for one of the most unpleasant afternoons of my life.

I would like the ARU and the SCG Trust to know that I, for one, have paid them my last dollar, and certainly I have made my last visit to watch their farcical entertainment in these disgusting conditions.

I am, or have been, a staunch follower of Rugby Union for 30 years, but after my last experience I will not be returning unless convinced that Saturday's performance will not be repeated.

If all who feel as I do, and they must be legion, stay away from these promotions, perhaps the organisers will wake up.

Comment. Looking ahead, I do not recall when the pendulum swung back **towards** the customer. I seem to recall that the Bi-Centenary Celebrations in 1988 brought a change in attitude.

In any case, by the year 2024, as I see it, most businesses are very conscious of their Public Relations, and indeed lots of them have a Public Relations Department and Officers. Quite often, this works out for the customers.

HARD WORK AHEAD FOR WHITLAM

Now that the election is over, it might be expected that Prime Minister would have a somewhat easier time ahead. **But, no, I do not think so.**

One reason for this doubt is that he will now reap the results of his pre-election manoeuvres. **Prior**, he presented a facade that said that the nation is doing pretty well, and the future is rosy-ish. **Post**, he had just been forced to tell a Premiers' Conference that Australia's trading position, relative to other nations, was shaping badly. And that all nations were heading for a bad time.

And that, in particular, our balance of payments problems might force us to borrow heavily. And, finally, that we as a nation would have to suffer austerities.

This was a sombre picture, vague though it might be. On top of that, he was frustrated by having finished the election with **a hung Parliament** that would delay, frustrate, even defeat his legislative plans. And loitering, now in the foreground, the multitude of problems associated with galloping inflation.

He was in the comfortable position of having no challenge to his leadership. He still had control of the House. It was just that something of his personal aura was slipping, and that some of his followers now saw him more as a **saviour**, rather than a **Saviour**.

We might keep an eye on this shift as we proceed.

JULY NEWS ITEMS

Mr Whitlam and Mr Crean (the Treasurer) have now **imposed a credit squeeze** that is affecting all aspects of borrowing and credit. And that, as part of inflation gripping the nation, is forcing prices up....

But there is a silver lining. If you want a second-hand big beast of a car, like a Falcon, Fairmont, Kingswood or Valiant Ranger, now is the time to buy. Because credit is hard to get, **the price of these has fallen** about 20 per cent in a week....

But credit is hard to get. The Motor Traders Association says "the Credit Companies **won't accept just anyone these days**. The person seeking credit must be a **gilt-edged risk.**"

The Government also announced that **interest rates on home loans will rise by a cool two per cent**, to an even cooler 10 per cent....

Think about it. Paying a mortgage rate of eight per cent already, **the rate is increased to ten per cent overnight. Mr Whitlam and Mr Crean won no friends on this matter,** no matter how you explain it.

One final report on the economy - for now. Dozens of big employers across the nation were **firing hundreds or thousands of workers**. And the Minster for Overseas Trade, Jim Cairns, announced **restrictions on many popular goods imported** from overseas....

One after the other, and more to come. Times in Australia were about to get a lot tougher.

Australia has declared that colour TV will be introduced in the next few months. Makers from Japan, England and America are scrambling to set up factories in Oz.

Australia's car production was shared between Holden, Ford and Chrysler. And also British Leyland. This latter company was small by comparison, but it was significant. It made, for example, **the Mini and Oxford**....

An enquiry by the Government's Industry Assistance Commission **suggested that Leyland cease production of cars in Australia**. That might mean that the remaining three makers would each get more of the market, and **avoid sackings. The Minister for Labour and Immigration thought this was a good idea**....

Leyland did not. South Australia did not. Trade Unions did not. Car buyers did not. But in any case, the very suggestion that Leyland might leave **sent its sales into a spin**....

"Great work", all you boffins in Canberra.

At the same time, **Japanese cars** were at **the beginning** of their penetration and **ultimate domination** of the market. These vehicles were not manufactured in Australia, they were imported as finished products, or in parts that were simply put together here.

There were a few commentators saying that we were **destined to become coolies**, simply buying and selling Japanese goods, and owning nothing ourselves.

WHITLAM'S FIRST AUSTERITY MOVES

It did not take Whitlam long to announce some of his austerity measures. By the end of the month, he had included:

No extra revenue assistance **grants for the States.**

Mail and telephone charges will rise.

Government **capital works spending** will be stringently curbed.

The **subsidy on petroleum products** sold in the country will be abolished.

Growth of the Commonwealth Public Service will be limited to 2.6 per cent.

The Army will not get 135 helicopters.

Civilian workers in the Defence Department will be reduced.

Comment. Nothing epic here, but a guide to what may come soon. Most Premiers thought that unemployment would rise, some talked about adding new consumer Taxes. Trade Union leader Bob Hawke growled a bit but rolled with the punches.

But, breathe a sigh of relief, **no Income Tax increases or the like.**

SINATRA BACK IN TOWN

Frank Sinatra flew into Melbourne to start a third tour of Australia. At one performance there, to a live audience of 7,000 people, he attacked the Press coverage he was getting, and included that Australian journalists were "parasites who had never done a day's work in their lives." He described women journalists as hookers and broads. He also scuffled with a few members of the Press.

Trade Unions objected to all this. After several hours of conferences, they said that they would not refuel his aeroplane. He had enough petrol to fly to Sydney. He did that, and slept the night there.

The President of the ACTU, Bob Hawke, representing the Union movement, said "He will never get out of Australia." This was on Thursday night.

On Friday morning, after hours in conference with Bob Hawke, now in Sydney, the Unions and the Sinatra team half-apologised to each other and announced that the "parties had reached an honourable settlement for both sides." Mr Hawke got some good headlines for "saving the Sinatra tour".

COMMENT

Sinatra has had an increasingly uncomfortable relationship with the Press as the years roll by. He has done nothing particularly bad, but he has got to the stage where the Press is always ready the take the Mickey out of him. This is true overseas, as well as in Australia.

Right now, in Australia, most readers of our Press would suspect that he has been offensive to journalists and might think of him as a punk.

But some people, some with more knowledge than most of us, thought differently.

Letters, T Morgan. Sinatra's visit to Australia proves at least one thing to the world. He may not be the best singer, but he certainly is the world's best promoter; an actor who is worth millions of dollars and never stops cashing in on his acting talents.

Good luck, Frankie! You have received colossal news coverage and fantastic free publicity; the fools are suckers to swallow your bait and you must be laughing all the way to the bank.

Never try to out-promote a promoter!

Letters, R Loblay. The reaction of the Unions to Mr Sinatra's behaviour is a clear example of the anarchy which is rapidly becoming a way of life in Australia.

Mr Sinatra's comments may well have been insulting and in poor taste, but they were clearly provoked by a stubborn press. Let each individual make a judgment about Mr Sinatra as a man, but how dare the Unions set themselves above the law in obstructing the freedom of speech and liberty to travel of any individual.

Not only have thousands of people been robbed of the opportunity of seeing Mr Sinatra perform - a once in-a-lifetime opportunity for most - but in the eyes of the world, Australia's image as an intolerant and immature society must be reinforced by our reaction.

The Unions' behaviour in this incident is far more offensive to me as an Australian than Mr Sinatra's, and adds to my, and many others', increasing irritation with the irresponsible industrial lawlessness and disregard for the people of this country which the Unions are manifesting.

A Union should be a democratically elected body representing the views of its members and ensuring satisfactory working conditions. Becoming judge, jury and executioner on political, social and environmental issues is a blatant misuse of power and is leading our country rapidly towards anarchy.

Who is running this country - a small group of power-hungry Union bosses or our democratically elected representatives?

The jury is still out for me. He might or might not be rough on journalists, but they seem able to defend themselves.

It might not matter. If it was convenient, and if I had the chance of going to see him perform, I would surely go. Even if I believed him to be all the bad things that the Press allege.

FAIR GO FOR MOTOR CYCLISTS

Below is a **contrarian** Letter which supports a view not often enunciated.

Letters, S Dearnley. In all the discussion that goes on about overcrowding on our urban roads, one mode of transport is almost always overlooked; the much maligned and misunderstood motor cycle.

The very word too often evokes an image of black-jacketed Visigoths, bemedalled with ersatz Iron Crosses, burning blue smoke in mobs down Main Street. The reality is more likely to be a slightly nervous commuter defensively riding a machine scarcely heavier than himself, taking up very little road space and burning a minimum of petrol on his way to town amid a throng of selfish individuals each piloting a ton or more of expensive and extravagant metal.

As a compensation, the motor cyclist enjoys a freedom that his hermetically sealed car-contained colleague can never know. He arrives at work glowing and fresh: on the way home he blows away the cares and cobwebs of the daily grind. (I write, with feeling, as a middle-aged rider who wishes he'd taken up this mode of transport years ago.)

But the stigma of the "bikie" image is hard to eradicate. Apart from the chiacking of one's friends, and the danger from the unthinking idiot who cuts across your bows as if you weren't there, even the Department of Motor Transport has it in for the poor motor cyclist.

For a 350cc bike (the ideal size for comfortable commuting) it charges $61.20 for registration and third-party insurance. This is as much as a car which is five times as heavy, takes up four times the space and chews up three times the amount of petrol.

Modern motor cycles are not the bangers of yesterday; they are not vehicles for inebriates or dimwits; they are far more sparing of natural resources than a car.

Give them a fair go!

Comment. There were many writers who thought differently. They considered bikies as dangerous, noisy bullies, and scary. They were smelly, and unkempt.

But, most of all, was their formation of clubs that were associated with crime. Crime that involved bashings, warfare, drugs, shoot-outs, organised crime and even murder.

Comment from middle class suburbia in 2024. But generally, people were prepared to give them a fair go, give them time to grow up. And indeed, most of them have. The weekend riders intent on freedom and fun, are very careful of their public image, and ride responsibly.

The problem with law-breaking bikie gangs still remains, perhaps worse, because they have progressively got more organised and more profitable.

NIXON: TIME IS UP

The US Congress was being besieged from all sides to settle once and for all whether President Nixon had breached any laws in his Watergate dealings. It appointed a House Committee to investigate the matter, and it eventually held a number of public hearings.

The end point of this Committee was whether it would make a recommendation to impeach Nixon. Generally, this Committee was a very partisan entity, with both Parties voting en bloc along Party lines.

But this time, it was different. As the hearings went on, it was becoming clear that a number of Republicans, Nixon's supposed supporters, would vote against him. Nixon could protest to assure voters that he was not guilty, but to no avail.

On July 28, the Committee voted 27 -11 to impeach Nixon. Over the next week, it was becoming clear that if Nixon was tried by impeachment, then he would be convicted.

So, he beat them to the punch. On August 10, he sat before an audience of 22 million TV viewers and told the world that he was resigning as President, He regretted doing so, he professed again his innocence. But the nation was being crippled by this controversy, and it was his reluctant duty to leave the Presidency.

Gerald Ford was chosen as his successor. One of his first decrees was that Nixon should be immune from prosecution for any of his actions.

Comment. I have no idea just how complicit Nixon was in the entire scandal. But he clearly did become involved to some extent and for some time. Whether his complicity warranted the harsh judgement that fell on him is not a matter for me to decide on.

Comment two. Without influencing judgements on the above paragraph, I add that 69 Nixon associates were found to be guilty in the sordid affair, and punished by the State accordingly.

FROM THE DINING-ROOM TABLE

It is now about half-way through the year. It's time to take stock, and sum up a little.

Householders, Mums and Dads, ordinary people in their own homes, were disgruntled. It seemed that, through no fault of their own, everything was against them. The obvious first thing was inflation. It had just been announced to have **risen to 16 per cent in the last quarter**. That meant that home mortgages would rise, and everything would cost more. .

Jobs were not so secure, and overtime was drying up. Strikes were constantly upsetting family schedules, and preventing travel, to school, sporting fixtures, work, and for amusement.

Our politicians had just held an election that had settled nothing. There were no changes in policy, virtually no changes in Cabinet, nothing new on the horizon to get excited about.

In the broader world, belief in the US had reached an all-time low, and the very basics of democracy were under examination. This nation's balance of payments were hardly adequate, and there was much talk about the extent that we should borrow from overseas. The world seemed to be headed for a Depression, and if so, our position would suffer.

At the local level, the newspapers were full of grizzles and complaints. This is always so, but now, there was a big spike. Everyone had a beef, or a feeling of unease. Take these two Letters as typical.

Letters, C Bass. N Eliades's complaint of the scarcity of school trousers brings forward yet another reason for an inquiry into the present-day cost and necessity of school uniforms.

The arguments for and against are perennial, often unreasoned and emotional, but parents should no longer ignore the fact that the **monopoly, of large business houses in school clothing, is nothing less than a racket**. It would appear that this monopoly is supported by schools themselves.

For example, when it is possible to buy men's woollen jumpers for $6 or $7 in large department stores, why should parents have to pay $11 to $15 for a school jumper of inferior quality, and in a colour (agreed upon by school and manufacturer) which can't be found in knitting wool?

Why do schools demand "regulation" black shoes for both sexes when they are so often unsuitable for out-of-school wear? At $10 to

$12 a pair, most parents can ill afford them. Is there connivance between schools and manufacturers here too?

Children are required by schools to over-dress in the heat of summer and under-dress in winter (primary school children are the only members of our community who are denied the comfort of long pants).

With the growing freedom in education, a world shortage of merchandise, and the outrageous prices of school uniforms, it is ridiculous to have to dress our children in unnecessary ties, hats, gloves, panty-hose which ladder quickly, and so on, when cheaper and more practical clothing is readily available and worn by our children anyway.

Finally, to the unfortunate child who does not conform to the "regulation" school uniform, subtle - and not-so-subtle - pressures are applied by school staff. There are no grounds on which such pressures can legally be applied, which leads one to suspect that,in the drab grey and navy world of the Australian classroom, it is the adults, not the students, who need the security of this expensive conformity.

Letters, R Brown. P Nankivell is not alone in being annoyed that she can buy woollen blankets only in pairs, not singly.

I too want only one blanket for my double bed and, because wool is fire resistant, I want wool.

But it seems that I shall have to buy a synthetic blanket, because I have no room to store an unused double blanket for the next umpteen years.

I just hope that all the other makers of goods don't decide to sell all their goods packaged in twos in the near future, because I'm also in the market for a new washing machine!

So let me sum up. It seems to me that the Whitlam honeymoon is coming to an end. Unless Whitlam can find a way to energise the population, to fill them with more hope for the future than they have right now, he might well be doomed.

Then again, I have been wrong in the past. We should keep an eye of developments, and sum up again in December.

HEROISM AT SEA

Letters, T Williamson. As a boating man, possibly more aware of the perils of the sea than most laymen, I pay my respects to the officers and men of HMAS Swan who spent a recent weekend on rescue missions in the most shocking conditions of hurricane-force (plus) winds and seas.

In particular I commend the three naval men who dived into the boiling sea at night in a 75-knot-plus wind, swam to and made possible the rescue of three men in a disabled craft. They did this with obvious disregard for their own safety. They could well have died in the attempt.

The seamanship displayed by the captain and crew in manoeuvring the Swan into position in these terrible conditions to effect the rescue, and the gallantry of the three who dived into the sea, speak most highly for the fine discipline and sense of duty which have always been so typical of the Australian serviceman when the pressure is really on.

Comment. In the hustle and bustle of our daily lives, we often forget that great deeds are sometimes unsung, and we know nothing of them. The above is a timely reminder of just that.

AUGUST NEWS ITEMS.

Milk prices in Sydney will rise by 13 per cent. Meat pies will rise by 10 percent, up to about 25 cents. Bread will rise by 2 cents per loaf - again.....

The *Sydney Morning Herald* is running photos of the Warringah Expressway, one of Sydney's main highways, showing that it was empty at noon yesterday. This was, because of strikes, **Sydney motorists had run out of petrol....**

The stock market continued its very sharp drop....

170,000 workers will be stood down because of a Transport Workers strike. The latest unemployment figures for July showed a drop in employment of 10,000....

There was plenty of misery to go round.

A police officer in the Queensland Drug squad had been giving druggies and surfies a hard time. It is believed that they sought revenge by setting up a **booby trap in an empty house** nearby....

A three-year-old girl wandered into the house and opened a cupboard. The gelignite bomb exploded and **blasted her across the room** and through a plate-glass window. She died on her way to hospital. The bomb was loaded with nuts and nails that would act as shrapnel.

The Federal Government had offered the Pilots Federation a pay increase **of 27 per cent**, but withdrew the offer after more squabbles. Politicians were in Canberra, so the **pilots banned all air travel to and from Canberra....**

The Government called on the RAAF to fly politicians both ways. An expensive way to move a few people to Sydney, Melbourne and Adelaide.

As the month progressed, bad economic news poured out. **The Government was clearly under stress**, and Ministers were proposing different and conflicting advice....

There were rumours that Whitlam would resign. There were comments from Minister Cameron that said the nation was in a state of anarchy. There were claims that the **link between Bob Hawke** and the ACTU, **and the Government**, were severely broken....

At the end of the month, in a special broadcast to the nation, **Whitlam tried to allay its fears.** In a speech that will be remembered only for its lack of any new information, **he failed to do that....**

In the next few days, it was reported that **new bank lending had fallen 60 per cent on a year ago.** And within two weeks, Public Opinion Polls showed a **two-week drop of 10 per cent in support for Labor nation-wide.**

August was a dreadful month for Labor. And the nation.

A WIN FOR LABOR

When it comes to elections, Australia is divided into geographical areas called electorates. That is, more-or-less permanent boundary lines are drawn, and each of these has about 70,000 persons of voting age in them. The idea of this is that every person's vote has the same value. "One man, one vote."

But over time, people move homes from place to place. For example, the drift to the cities. If a city suburb becomes crowded, but the electoral boundaries remain the same, then the value of a resident's vote therein drops. That is not fair, so the boundaries change.

In Australia, all electoral boundaries are reviewed about every five years. There is always a bun fight between the Parties about where these new boundaries should be. **In the long run**, it is Parliament that votes to accept or reject the suggestions put forward.

This time, Whitlam was frustrated. By now he had put forward, on three separate occasions, suggestions for social changes, and each time they had been rejected by the Senate. This, it seemed could go on forever. And there were five other bits of legislation that were also rejected three times.

He and his advisers exercised a **brave plan that had never been done before in our history**. He approached the High Court of Australia, and got its permission to hold **the sitting of a joint session of Parliament**, in which the two Houses sat in a single Chamber, and voted as a single body.

Whitlam had a majority on this basis, and the six matters were passed into law.

Importantly, he now had control of both Houses, because if the Senate in future did reject any proposals, it knew that a joint sitting could be held, and the rejection would be pointless.

That is, Whitlam removed the spectre of the Senate blocking future legislation passed up from the House.

This was a real win for Whitlam and left him free to get on with his job.

TRIBUTES TO NIXON

Most Letter writers were happy to see Nixon go. He had earned himself a number of enemies over his tardiness in getting out of the Vietnam War. On top of that, his conduct during the Watergate years had robbed him of the deference that he might otherwise expect.

But he had his supporters, and one of these stands out.

Letters, E White (Sir Ernest White was co-founder of the Australian-American Association, and President of the Association 1967-1968.). Another Jesus Christ is about to be crucified. Laugh if you will. But the pious and sanctimonious are about to crucify President Nixon because he chose to try and protect his stupid and ill-advised staff from their own actions.

The fact that he brought about peace in Vietnam, brought about detente with China and Russia, and thereby stopped Russia going to war with China and vice versa, and stopped the Egyptian-Israel war which could possibly have flared into a world war, means nothing to the American people.

No one approves of his misleading statements but **there was a good, human Christian excuse, viz. to help his immediate staff out of trouble**. Good and bad cannot and never will be expressed in sharp good or bad and it is pious and hypocritical nonsense to suggest they can.

We crucify President Nixon for **a little bad** and give him no credit for **the great good** and in doing so we clear the road for Russia and Communism to forge ahead as she is in the Baltic States.

We hold up our hands to high heaven about his tax misdemeanours, overlooking the fact that all great entities had in the past delivered their records to the State and been duly credited, and in any case it was a matter of date not dishonesty.

That great and good man of his time Jesus Christ was crucified. Why? Because he became hated in fear of his powers - among which he or his followers claimed that he walked on water, turned stone into bread, etc. - but among his followers he only had one Judas. President Nixon has a whole army of Judases.

He has shown outstanding fortitude and courage, and now his enemies are coming in for the kill adding insult to injury suggesting he is mentally unbalanced. Would to God we had a few more unbalanced like him on earth for world peace has now been put in the discard.

Letters, Melita Lawton. Mr Nixon gets no credit at all from me for his part in the Vietnam War. He could have stopped the War fully when he took office in 1969. But he did not. Instead he grandstanded and played the world stage for years, and to get maximum political kudos from reluctantly stopping it.

That is after thousands of extra American, and thousands of Vietnam civilians, were pointlessly killed.

And hundreds of our boys, including my son.

He gets no credit from me.

Letters, Arthur Barns. If a job applicant told me that he lied and obfuscated on some matters, I would not employ him. Even if he added that he was loyal to his colleagues.

If he was applying for President for the United States, and that meant he would take many oaths and swear many times to adhere to the values of the US. If he said he lied daily, and would do so for year after year, I still would not employ him. Even if he said he was loyal to his colleagues.

If it turned out that he could use his high position to connive with 100 top Washington aids to lie and obfuscate, I would not employ him. No matter that he was loyal to his mates. **That is how I feel about Nixon.**

STRIKE FIRST: APOLOGIA

Everyone in Australia hates strikes. They make life for the ordinary family uncertain, uncomfortable, and sometimes unhealthy.

Yet every person working for a wage is inclined to themselves strike over wages or conditions. It could be that they think that **their** strike is just, and that all others are not. It could be that the world will realise the justice of **their** grievances, and that they will be forgiven from the strictures placed on **others**.

But that is not the reality. People strike because **there is no other way**, at the moment, to get a fair hearing of their claims, and a reasoned chance of revision.

Take this Letter as an example.

Letters, P Cocks. How quick we are to criticise the Unionists for ignoring arbitration channels and supporting their wage claims with strike action.

Having been closely associated with an application for a new award before the Industrial Commission of NSW, I can now understand why many Unions have rejected our arbitration system. The award to which I refer expired in June, 1973, was mentioned before a Conciliation Commissioner in December last and then referred to the Commission. The hearing commenced in April of this year and concluded last month, after numerous delays. A decision is still awaited.

Meanwhile, Unions **taking strike action**, have their cases referred for **immediate** arbitration and early decision. The disadvantages of having taken the correct course include excessive time delay, an altered political and economic climate in which the decision is to be handed down and no guarantee of retrospectivity.

An increasing number of my colleagues have expressed disillusionment with the current arbitration system and when next this award expires, it will be difficult to persuade the majority that there are real advantages to be gained by going to arbitration rather than taking industrial action.

Let me continue. Proponents **for** strikes say that, at the moment, inflation is running at 16 per cent per annum. In the circumstances outlined in the above Letter, who wants to delay for two years, and wait for a mysterious tribunal to hand down a dubious judgement. And that judgement, however just or not just, would be binding for another few years.

Surely, they say, it is better to strike **now** for **their** benefits, and lock in whatever a strike will bring them.

They might go on: As for the other claims by **other strikers,** they are outrageous, and it is **they** who should use the arbitration system and stop the strikes.

Comment. It is becoming obvious that inflation is laying bare the weakness in the slowness of arbitration. And, to be fair, authorities across the nation are now talking again at a faster rate, about how to fix this.

The President of the ACTU, Bob Hawke, has got this particular bit between his teeth, and will continue to press for changes.

But this will take time, so **what option do you have now**?

FOSTER CHILDREN IN SOCIETY

Letters (Mrs) B Cullen, Vice-President, 1974 Child Care Week Committee. The news that **31 residents** of Walker Avenue, St Ives, **have protested** at the proposal of the Church of England to accommodate foster parents and 10 children in the area makes one feel ashamed to belong to the human race.

Have they no concern for children in care? Is all compassion dead? If a family with 10 children of its own moved in, would they then object? If not, what is the difference?

Do they not realise that there, but for the grace of God, go their children? Do they not subscribe to the United Nations Declaration on the Rights of the Child?

To say that 10 children will reduce the value of their properties is nonsense. However, one must pity people who have such a false sense of values, and hope that their consciences will cause them to withdraw their objections, and that the Council will come down on the side of those who are making constructive efforts to give children the chance to become good citizens.

Comment. It is regrettable, but true, that there were many people who looked with distaste on foster children, and on the provision of care for the unfortunate youngsters. There was no factual doubt that, wherever they were placed, the delinquency rate was higher. And, sad to say, many of the children graduated quickly to crime and gaols.

It is understandable that many residents of leafy, wealthy St Ives would not take the risk of a foster home nearby. Also, at a time when children still played in the streets, who would choose to have their children do that with their new neighbours.

Yet many of the occupants of the gracious homes in St Ives have hearts of gold. They would see the absolute necessity of providing foster care and accommodation somewhere. Why not take a fair share of that themselves?

And some would argue that, **if foster homes were located in better places**, then maybe the end-product would be improved. Change the environment, change the result.

There are many other sides to this argument. **Where is Solomon when you need him?**

GIVE US A BREAK, DOCTOR JIM

Doctor Jim Cairns was soon to become this nation's Treasurer. He was always a maverick, and outspoken on matters outside his existing portfolio (Trade).

Thus no one was surprised when he spoke up on the finance of the nation. What did surprise quite a few was that he claimed that people were better off now than they were a year ago.

Letters, B Brownrigg. As the most irresponsible statement of the week I nominate Dr Cairns' claim that there was hardly a person in Australia, with the possible exception of stock and real estate speculators, not better off now than 12 months ago.

Doesn't Dr Cairns know, or care, about the thousands of elderly, retired people on small fixed incomes sinking hopelessly in the quicksand of inflation?

These are the people let down so callously by the Government's off-hand decision not to keep its much-repeated promise in the September Budget to abolish the means test for the 70-74s.

And these are the people who are suffering most through the effects of the Government's spendthrift policy, excessive wage demands and reckless strikes which have put the nation's economy on the skids.

Letters, A Thomas. So Dr Cairns, from his Ivory Palace in Canberra, with taxpayers' money creating his pay packet, opines that there can hardly be any one not better off than he was 12 months ago. What stupendous tripe.

As a retired person on strictly limited means my only asset increasing in value with inflation is the family home. This is only a relative thing and benefits me not at all.

My small investments diminish daily in power to buy requirements. I was self-employed and sold my modest business two years ago on terms. Imagine what is happening to the value of the instalments owing to me, not to mention the rate of interest then thought reasonable.

Perhaps there are one or two others in the community who do not feel better off.

Letters, Frankie Fain. Even if Cairns was right, that would be only part of the story.

The damage that this Government is inflicting on this nation has only just started to bite. **There is a lot more to come in the next many years.** When that happens, will Cairns still be keen to advertise his views?

COMMENT ON UNIONS

Letters, W Scotford. On the surface our legislators appear unable to agree on the steps necessary to avoid chaos. They consistently refuse to face and admit the obvious, namely that Unions, like all other units in our society, must be bound by rules defining the mean by which they may achieve their objectives. These rules should require that they take their claims to a tribunal, which would decide the issues in accordance with economic guidelines presented by the Government.

In the meantime we approach a state of chaos enthroned, leading to unemployment, depression and possible anarchy.

DELINQUENCY IN SCHOOLS

This, of course, was not a new problem. Every teacher knows that there will always be some nitwit or rebel who will be disruptive. Whatever the class, whatever the reason, whatever the fix, there is always one or more in every class.

But the problem now was that the disrupters were growing in number, they were often extending their bad behaviour to violence towards other students and to teachers, and often were getting support from their parents.

There were many people who were addressing this problem. One solution was to say the problem had its roots in the home. Fix that, and delinquency would go away.

Others said the problem was that **children were forced to go to school**. Some children were certain to rebel against this. This rebellion shows up as delinquency at school. **Let children leave school at any age**, and the problem will go away. **Surely.**

One writer puts a good argument against this. "Would it not be a case of **moving delinquency from the schools to the streets**. Our ancestors fought for more than a century to get children out of factories and coalmines; now our modern day educators want to put the children back."

Another suggestion comes from the observation that delinquency correlates with failure to master the basics in reading and writing . **Teach them to read and write.** Problem solved. That was simple, really.

But, as you can readily see, how do you do this if the children will not listen and learn.? To exaggerate, how do you insert knowledge into children who are already busy punching heads?

Whatever the solution, the problem was acute.

Letters, K Oliver, Relieving principal, Rooty Hill High School. J Simon, principal, Nursery School Teachers' College, Newtown, must be joking or totally out of touch with reality when he claims that educators are not experiencing difficulties with the responsible and moral behaviour of students. There would be very few teachers or principals of schools who would endorse such a statement.

Only the way-out educators, or those with very permissive views, themselves, would deny that the lack of moral and social responsibility among our young people is one of the greatest problems facing educators today. Every social function is a social hazard and demands the utmost vigilance, because of the irresponsible and reckless behaviour of our youth.

In many classrooms the situation is fast reaching the point of being quite unbearable for the teacher. Insolence and defiance are the order of the day. Heartbroken, disillusioned and frustrated teachers are giving up in despair. These are the real reasons why teachers are resigning in such numbers and why the Department is having such difficulty in enticing young people into the teaching profession.

If principals of Teachers' Colleges and others in authority think these situations do not exist, let them spend more time at the battlefront and less in their remote isolation and comfort.

We are starving and destroying the spirit of our youth. We are reaping the fruits of anarchy and terror. Let those who share this concern cry out for a new direction in every area of educational thinking and planning.

Comment. On the other hand, writing in 2024, if you go to a graduation ceremony of children leaving school, look at the graduands. They are, almost all, beautiful, well-behaved, smart young people who are a tribute to the system that made them that way.

That is, **in my opinion**, alarmists aside, **the system overall is working well.**

But, **another suggestion**, what you might do is take all the humanity out of all people at all times. Maybe that will fix a few problems.

LANTANA ALERT

Those readers who are concerned about the lantana menace will find this interesting.

Comment.   A reply from the CSIRO pointed out that research into lantana was continuing, although it was necessarily a slow process. A particular danger with biological control was the introduction of some insect to get control, only to find that this insect became a menace to other plants.

Also a problem was growing the insect in sufficient numbers, and at appropriate locations, to satisfy demand.

Work is on-going although it was agreed, not at a pace fast enough.

Second comment.   Down the East Coast to Gosford, farmers will agree that, by 2024, the problem has not yet been solved.

SEPTEMBER NEWS ITEMS

Leonard Bernstein was conducting the Sydney Symphony Orchestra, playing the first movement a symphony by Tchaikovsky. **A baby cried** and spoilt the piece. **Bernstein then conducted it again**, much to the delight of the audience.

The laundry room at a Convent in Tasmania exploded and **killed seven people and critically injured 15 others**. The incident happened during the installation of a new boiler.

In August, Australia suffered its **worst Trade Gap** since 1951. **Unemployment grew by 26 per cen**t in that month. These figures are **bad enough** to worry even the most sanguine.

President Ford announced **a full pardon for ex-President Nixon** for his part in Watergate. He was granted a "full, free, and absolute pardon" for any acts he had committed....

Nixon admitted that he was wrong in not acting more swiftly and more decisively in dealing with Watergate. It was **his first admission of any part of the blame at all**. **58 per cent of the US population opposed** the granting of immunity from prosecution.

The *SMH* announced that in today's *Herald* a special feature will discuss how the **new Bankcard Credit Card system** will work, who can join, how much it will cost, and how much credit it will give you.

Believe it or not. Householders will get a break. The **licence fees for having a radio or TV will be abolished**. $8 and $20 respectively....

Until now, well-trained inspectors **cruised around suburbs and country towns looking for aerials** indicating possession. Then they would swoop and fine those owners who could not produce the annual licence....

The inspectors were ever-vigilant, visiting most areas **at least four times a year**.

A **soccer train** from London to Southhampton was trashed en-route by **315 passengers** on it. On arrival at Southhampton, **they were all arrested** and shipped off to various prison facilities, where they were held pending police enquiries.

A young married couple in NSW had applied months ago to adopt two Vietnamese children. Nothing special. Except that **the couple said they were agnostics.** That is, they did not believe in the Christian God....

Their application was not approved, and the matter was raised to the level of the NSW Supreme Court....

The Court found that **being agnostic did not impact the application**, and that the adoption could proceed.

The **Government introduced the Budget** for next year. It ignored the huge mess that the nation was headed for, and was quite moderate in its decisions. It did **introduce a new Capital Gains Tax** which has become a bugbear for many in later years.

MOTHERS' PLACE IS IN THE HOME

In this Section, I talk about the sending of very young children to another place for a part of the day. For example, perhaps they might go to a neighbour for two hours. Or they might go to a kindergarten for six hours.

I will take the easy way out by using the word "kinder" , knowing full well that the formal Kinder movement was hardly here by the mid-1980's.

It seems that about half the mothers in the nation **agree that** Mums should stay at home and mind the children. And **half of them do not**.

Certainly, a lot of them have already gone to work, and a lot more would like to. An equal cohort would say that to do so is to deprive children of all the joys that a young child and the mother should have, and is trundling the child into the harsh world before they are ready.

The two Letters below give the argument **in favour of staying at home**.

Letters, (Mrs) M Bexon. I am sure there are many women like myself, in the 50-plus age group, who deplore the present tendency among young mothers to want to place their infant offspring in kindergartens and child-minding centres, almost as soon as they leave the hospital maternity ward.

There has been much outcry by womenfolk for the Government to provide more facilities for pre-school children and, no doubt, they are heartened by the Prime Minister's statement this week that the Government is going ahead with a greatly expanded program in that direction.

While I do not dispute that there are certain instances where such child-minding facilities are a necessity - for unmarried mothers, in one-parent families, or in the case of an invalid father - I consider it a tragedy and a travesty of family life to suggest that young children below school age should go into kindergartens as a matter of course.

In my opinion, the rightful place for a child, until it reaches school age, is in the home in the loving care of its mother, and nothing can ever replace that which is its birthright. Even animals do not thrust their young from them until they have reached some degree of maturity. With modern methods of birth-control, most parents plan their families, so motherhood is not thrust upon the women of today as an inevitable, and sometimes unwelcome, duty as it was in the past.

So, young mothers, do not be too hasty to throw away those precious, all too fleeting, infant years. Better by far to manage without a few luxuries. When a baby-sitter is required for the odd emergency which arises, surely there is a willing friend able to mind your child with hers for a while, or a grandparent eager to look after junior for an hour or two. Then, when school arrives, if you are not the sort of person who likes making your own and your children's clothes, pottering in the garden, or thinking up new recipes, there are opportunities for part-time employment which would enable you to work during school hours.

Letters, (Mrs) S Wallace. Why all this fuss and bother about child care? I always thought child care was a mother's job - or have all the mums of Australia decided to abandon their kids en masse?

I was born into and grew up in a home, and, in turn, brought up my own children always believing that nothing mattered more than the safety, well-being and security of the family.

The latest idea seems to be for mums to dump their kids as soon as possible in the lap of some new-fangled, and costly, Government-sponsored child minding set-up, and forget them. What kind of young Australians are these institutions going to produce?

Isn't being a good wife and mother good enough for our women? Or has the once good and proud Australian "way of life" so deteriorated that both husband and wife **must** go out to work just to pay the bills, regardless of the neglect of children, of home life and family welfare this must inevitably involve? If so, God help Australia.

The arguments **for going to kinder** included that the range of activities and learning made the children happy, and it produced better-informed children. That they were almost always happy to go, and then come home to a mother. That the mother got a break, and that allowed for a happier home. That ignorance is always a bad thing, and keeping the child ignorant was not helping anyone.

There were many hypotheses, many of them not proven, but "obvious".

The general case for having the facility for child-minding centres is put below.

Letters, (Mrs) M Long. The letter from Mrs S Wallace appears to typify the reaction of many people to the Government's decision to re-implement their child-care scheme.

Mrs Wallace was lucky enough to have had a normal family life. However, this seems to have blinded her to the hard fact that some people are less fortunate.

Has she spared a thought for the children of one-parent families? How does she imagine a single parent being able to bring in enough money without taking a job? Has Mrs Wallace ever tried to support a family on a deserted wife's or widow's pension?

All the love in the world can't supply the necessary food and shelter for a child.

In the past the family unit was more compact. A child would often be cared for by relations while his single parent went out to work. However, nowadays, when so many young families are situated in big cities far away from any relation, there is nothing else to do when disaster strikes but fall back on child-care organisations.

I realise many parents might avail themselves unnecessarily of such a scheme. However, it is surely better to provide safe child-care facilities, no matter how newfangled or costly, for those needy single-parent families. Children of parents who can, but don't want to, keep them at home might conceivably be better off in such an environment, rather than have them stay at home and pick up feelings (so rapidly transmitted to young minds) of being a burden and unwanted by their parents.

God help Australia, if the majority of the population thinks so little of those less fortunate than themselves.

But below are **three** different opinions on the matter.

Firstly an argument from a woman who said that a number of women she knew were unfit to be mothers, and no child should be held at home with them 24-hours a day. She cited drunkenness, smoking, and laziness, and added houses in turmoil, and families in turmoil. How lucky a child was to escape, if only for a few hours a day, from that.

Secondly, some mothers want the extra money. They might want to move out of rented premises and buy a house of their own. For the family. They might want to take a holiday. For the family. They might want to save money to send their children later to a private school, For the family. Can anyone criticise these parents?

Thirdly, a mother wrote that she is surrounded by mothers with young children. They all tell her that she should, or she should not, send her children off to a kinder of some type.

She says that it is none of their business. There are many reasons, some of them might be seen as good, and some of them seen as bad. But only the parents can know what they are. Let people alone to make their own judgements.

"Get off my back."

Comment. This question, whether to send or not send, was **to worry families for decades**. As the kinder industry grew, and bigger establishments also became dominant, and as back-yarders gave way, **the question remained**. As the substitute Mums were replaced by graduates from colleges, all with tickets, **the question still remained**.

Now, in 2024, I suggest that it will always remain. Not so much in the Press as now, but **always in the minds of mothers and fathers** who are charged with having to make what is, for most, a really difficult decision.

HAPPENINGS IN THE SOAP INDUSTRY

I know you have been waiting anxiously for news of the soap industry. Here it is. Hot off the Press.

Letters, R Robertson. Your story, "Soap makers asked to justify claims" tells us that "please explain" questionnaires will be sent to soap companies by the Minister for Science, Mr Morrison.

A product, for washing clothes, hands or dishes, must perform its role effectively, and if it does not, it is simply not bought again. Performance is paramount and failure to perform is treated ruthlessly by the housewife.

Research also reveals another interesting fact. While the washing process is generally believed to be a mundane and pragmatic chore, research analysis proves otherwise. Washing is also a highly involving and emotional housewife responsibility. Like it or not, the housewife is assessed on her skill in that role by the tangible results visible to her family, her friends and her neighbours.

There are degrees of whiteness, Mr Morrison, and they do not only exist in the minds of advertising copywriters. They exist in practical reality when the neighbour looks over the fence on washday.

It is not "meaningless nonsense" to talk about lemons and blue beads... these are ingredients, they do perform and, most important, they do mean something to the housewife, something to which she can relate from her own personal experience.

Finally, research also shows another fallacy in the arguments always advanced in the quest for information. It is true that one of the most often repeated requests is for on-pack information about product ingredients. But a little further probing will show the evident fact that a listing of these ingredients is totally meaningless to the vast majority of the consumers.

Unless the housewife holds a science degree, does she know what perborate is? Or what percentage of opacifier is more economical? Or what effect, if any, does tri-poly-phosphate have on ecology? Useful information, Mr Morrison, but to whom?

Comment. To me, this Letter was a revelation. I particularly liked the bit about "washing is a highly involving and emotional housewife responsibility".

I remind you that this was written at a time when detergents were still making progress in the war against soaps.

THE ROLE OF CLUBS

Clubs have become an important part of the Australian social scene. If you go back 20 years, many clubs were devoted to activities, such as golf clubs and bowling clubs. At that time, too, there was a growing number of community clubs that catered for ex-servicemen and Workers. The boom that started then has kept growing, and most suburbs and country towns can now boast a club or two.

At the same time, and perhaps as a consequence, drinking habits changed a lot. Clubs began to cater for meals, and women, and social events, and community activities, and entertainment, and civilisation gradually came to the drinking scene. In many places.

One big event for the clubs was the introduction and promotion of poker machines. This source of revenue **to the clubs** gave them a big boost, and allowed them to **compete with pubs**. At the same time, as the number of clubs grew, and as the workforce turned more professional, Trade Unions came to the scene.

And with them came organised demands for increased wages and benefits. At the moment, such demands were being made to counter inflation. They ranged from about 20 per cent to about 30 per cent, depending what State you were in.

These were **so-called ambit claims** which many Unions made. That is, Unions asked for increases that were beyond their wildest dreams, and hoped that, after negotiations, they might get half of them.

But even so, claims of 25 per cent were close to crippling, especially for small clubs.

Letters, G Donovan. A recent wage increase of 28 per cent to many employees has caused some clubs to raise annual subscriptions by more than 60 per cent merely to meet the increased wage burden.

Most people agree that clubs play an important role in social life today. Nevertheless, if they are being placed continually under pressure by strikes, excessive wage demands and such like, many will have no option but to cease operations. In the interests of the community generally, the parties concerned should desist from their current demands, and consider what consequences will follow if the demands are pursued.

Comment. I find it hard to find any evidence that such calls for moderation had any effect.

Second Comment. As the years passed through the 1970's and beyond, a large number of clubs did respond to financial pressures **by closing down**. And perhaps half of them ceased operating, and bigger clubs took their place.

Third Comment. While I am an advocate for the small corner store, I think the bigger clubs have advantages that the small clubs do not. For example, bringing in Saturday night entertainers is possible only if the club is big enough. And, it is easier to provide a decent menu when the membership is larger.

OCTOBER NEWS ITEMS

Warning to Labor. In NSW, recent elections for local Councils showed a large swing away from Labor. Many votes went to Independents. But for **Labor at the Federal level, the results were alarming**.

Cambridge Credit was a leader in the personal finance lending business. If you wanted a loan for a car, or a washing machine, you went to just a few such companies, and they would lend to you at **a rate that was double the rate from a bank**. But in a world that was lavishly adopting the HP model of living, Cambridge Credit was tops....

It made its money **from borrowing** via debentures from the public. And then lending that money to others. But now, in these hard times and credit squeeze, **it could no longer borrow**....

So it announced **it would go into receivership**. That meant that people who had lent the money in the first place, had lost all....

It was a warning to **other companies in the industry** that their days were numbered. They did, in fact, **all fall in the next few months**. (And they took some of my money with them.)

There were "runs" on all finance companies following the receivership announcement. This was right across the nation, especially for HP companies....

In Adelaide, **Premier Dunstan** attended a HP company. **People were queuing to withdraw their** money. He addressed them with a loud hailer, and told them that their money was safe and there was no need to panic....

You all know what happens as soon as someone mentions the words "Don't panic...."

The Government said it would ease the credit squeeze "significantly". Spokesmen from everywhere assured the nation that institutions, like banks and Building Societies, were secure. The more authorities spoke thus, the more people got frightened....

As a result of the easing of credit, a few days later, the Stock Market recovered, and the "run" on the HP industry had stopped.

The Builders Labourers Federation Executive has decided that the NSW Branch should be dismantled, and a new Branch established. It claims NSW had gone too far in "green-banning" too many building projects....

For example, they had banned activity on eight sites worth $3,000 million in Sydney's CBD, and also a huge number in the rest of the City of Sydney, and in the State....

Jack Mundey, the NSW leader, says they will fight this....

Some irreverent journalists are talking about the possible dangers when thieves fall out.

PAGES OF LETTERS ON INFLATION

Inflation in September rose to 17 per cent per annum. That means that wages followed, cost of living followed, rents followed, and mortgages followed. Perhaps that sounds fair enough. After all, if everything moved up 17 per cent, then everyone ends up square.

You all know that is not the case. Some people do make a quid out of inflation (see Mr Baker's Letter below), and some lose a quid. Those who win do not say so. Those who lose, write to the Letters Pages of the Press.

Right now, with inflation bolting, the Letters poured in. The Press are devoting very large spaces to them, and they just keep coming.

Below is a sample from the losers. After that, I include a letter from Mr Baker that adds a different perspective.

Letters,W Parsons, S Powell, C Pearmain, P Pharaoh. We are disappointed at the lodging of wage claims pitched at far more than the amount actually expected. It would seem far better to show the public that we can be responsible by calculating the claim realistically, and sticking to that realistic claim rather than strengthening the belief that Unions are out for all they can get.

We do not believe in accelerating an already irrational and confused situation.

Letters, E McDonald. If my employees could see their Government providing the people of this country with some noticeable benefits, I am certain they would feel happier about the **amount of tax removed** from their pay packets each week. However, my staff are sufficiently realistic to see that this is a situation which must come to one inevitable conclusion. Before too long I, and others like myself, will be forced to close our businesses, and unemployment will face the many employees of small concerns.

Letters, M Bray. It is of course true that world-wide inflation is an international problem, to a great extent brought about by the energy crisis and sky-rocketing oil prices. What is not mentioned, though, is that the Whitlam Government has largely succeeded in destroying a strong and healthy Australian economy in just 18 months, without the help of increased oil prices - the price of Australian crude is still at 1971 levels.

Letters, R Jackson. The Prime Minister's call for restraint has a hollow ring. When new in office, he set the pace in the wages and salaries scramble by large hand-outs to the Commonwealth Public Service. The private sector was quick to follow. The consequences of this we see today.

It is as simple as that!

Maybe if wages could be winched back to levels of "pre-December-1972", prices would quickly follow. No stores are marking-up for fun - the shop assistants are just too expensive to employ and one large chain store has just closed 36 branches, due to excessive wage bills.

As far as Australia is concerned, it is time the blame was allocated to the culprits responsible for today's inflation. They call themselves "The Australian Government." May the Lord have mercy on us all!

Letters, M Ringland. During this term, students will be thinking about a career. For those of you that are overweight may I suggest teaching, as trainee allowances this year have been on a poverty level. I have lost more than a Stone in a term (12 weeks) and still don't have enough to live on.

In times of galloping inflation, others may take heart from the minister's stand of refusing to add to the inflationary trend by giving us enough to live on.

Now the Letter from Mr Baker. I can't guarantee his figures are exact, but they are close enough to make his point.

Letters, M Baker. With inflation, you would think from the Letters columns that everyone is a loser. That is not the case.

Take the man with a mortgage and the ability to pay the increase. Then his living costs go up, but so too does his salary. Enough to cover the increased cost.

His mortgage payment goes up, but nowhere near the 17 per cent because his loan is taken out over 30 years. In fact, it will go up about 20 per cent **of the mortgage payment**.

But the value of his property will go up about 17 per cent.

Every year he benefits by 17 per cent, if inflation stays high. What a cop. **Inflating his way out of debt.**

It is true, that others are losers. People paying rent for example. But my point is that it is not realistic to say the every one loses under inflation. **A large number are laughing their way to the bank.**

WHO JUDGES THE POLICE?

Mr Buckley below responded to a number of events where **police were involved but required further investigation of their actions**. For example, where the police are confronted by an armed offender who presents a material threat to their lives, and is shot by the police. Clearly there must be an investigation, but the question was, **who** was to conduct this?

Letters, K Buckley, President, Council for Civil Liberties. The State Government's decision to establish an independent tribunal concerning complaints about police is welcome in principle. Whether the new system will prove satisfactory in practice depends upon details of its working which have not yet been announced.

The "Herald" Editorial says that the police force will retain its right of initial investigation of complaints against its members, but that where there is evidence that the police probe had been unsatisfactory, the matter can be referred to the new tribunal. This implies merely an ex post facto review - an independent check after the police have investigated and rejected a complaint.

Mr Buckley goes on to discuss how other States and nations handle this question.

His Letter raises the difficulty of finding a suitable way to adjudicate these matters. Everyone agrees that **an outside body**, independent of the police immediately involved, should be used. But how independent should it be?

Police from the same Station? Police from outside? A special police squad? Police at all? If not, who? Local magistrates? A special tribunal?

There are arguments for all of these. And against.

And in any case, what guarantee is there of an impartial decision? Attitudes to the police vary so much in society that many judgements are made long before any evidence is presented. **Even an outside independent tribunal cannot convincingly say that it is not swayed by the Press**, by public opinion, and political persuasion.

The question remained, who is to investigate the police?

Comments. Let us jump ahead to 2024, fifty years later. In a most controversial situation, police in NSW were called to an aged care home in the middle of the night. There they were confronted by a woman with a knife. One officer tasered her, and she died a few days later. This woman was in fact 95-years-old, and widely thought of as being no threat to the police.

The question became , who was to investigate the conduct of the police? **It turned out that there was no protocol that satisfied any one.** The Press and many citizens were baying for police blood. Many others were saying that decisions should be made only after the facts were clear. **The police themselves were refusing to present the facts.**

So, back to 1974.

The situation in 2024 is no different from that in 1974. **Fifty years earlier**, the same questions were bedevilling the population. **Namely, who should investigate the police?**

Second comment. Generally, in looking at 2024 and 1974, it is easy to see that times have changed things and many attitudes. But here is one public opinion where nothing has changed. In my reading **I found that the arguments brought forth in 2024 are almost identical to those in 1974. Maybe there *is some* truth to the truism that "Some things never change".**

REFORM OF DIVORCE RULES

Whitlam had come to Government with the promise that he would reform the nation's laws on divorce. Firstly, he would make them uniform, so that the same laws would apply no matter what State the appellants were in.

But equally important, he promised that the substance of the Act would also change. Now, the new proposed legislation is about to start its tortuous way through Parliament.

Here is an appreciation of some of its features.

Letters, B Marshall and 7 others. As members of the Commission on the Status of Women of the Australian Council of Churches (NSW), we wish to express our support for the proposed Family Law Bill, and welcome it as compassionate and humane legislation.

Implicit within its provisions is the acknowledgment that marriage is essentially a voluntary union, both at the time of legal contracting and for the duration of the relationship.

The concept of "irretrievable breakdown of marriage" as the one and only ground for divorce reflects the understanding that when relationships fail blame is obscure and impossible to identify.

As members of the Christian Church we applaud the elimination of "fault" with its emphasis on guilt and punishment, and we welcome the provision for partners to share the responsibility of breakdown as they would share the responsibility and joy of success.

We also welcome the measures taken to ensure the protection of rights and welfare of the children of the marriage, and look forward to the provision of closed family courts free from the traumatising effect of traditional legal regalia and procedure.

The intention to reduce legal costs is most commendable.

We would like to convey to the Attorney-General, and those responsible for this proposed legislation, our support of the Family Law Bill and our recognition of it as positive legislation aimed at reducing human suffering and emphasising the worth and dignity of persons.

Comment. The end product will be a bit different, and cover more than this Letter. But it will be seen as a vast improvement over the previous versions of the States' Acts, and will be greeted with a sigh of relief by the vast majority.

MENTAL ILLNESS *IS* AN ILLNESS

I include this Letter on a matter I have rarely touched on in writing my 36 books in this Series. One reason for this neglect has been that readers in 1974, and before, rarely wrote Letters to the Press **about mental health as such.**

They did write a little about mental health **institutions**, but almost nothing about the personal effects. And the Press, like everyone else, wished it under the carpet. So too did I.

Letters, "Psychiatric Patient". I am a psychiatric patient, and find that using brand X of soap will not wash away a disturbed mind. The trouble with psychiatric patients is that they appear normal physically, and there is no way of showing the public the mental suffering which they experience. The public give compassion to the physical sufferer, but just tells the psychiatric patient to "pull up his socks and stop brooding." How the unfortunate sufferer would like to be able to do this! Most fellow psychiatric patients agree with me that they would prefer to suffer a broken limb than their mental anguish.

As a single girl who would like to be married, I was very hurt by a boyfriend who left me because "you always seem to be sick." Would he have made this cruel remark to a physically handicapped person?

Other cruel remarks made which stigmatise the psychiatric patient include "drive me up the wall," "nearly go mental," "looney bin," "crackers," "bonkers," etc. Are there any equivalent "jokes" stigmatising physically handicapped people?

Employment is difficult for a psychiatric patient, as is obtaining life assurance. Interviews for employment are a great strain, as the patient must hide his past for fear of the employer considering the patient too unstable for the position. I have been refused life assurance by one of Australia's largest life assurance companies because I have had a nervous breakdown.

In the wonderful psychiatric unit of a leading public hospital which I attend, emphasis is given to boosting the morale of patients by encouraging them to take care of their appearance - i.e. by choosing between brands X and Y of lipstick, etc. However, I feel that the more attractive a patient appears, the more likely he or she is to appear normal and thus receive less sympathetic understanding.

My letter may also appear to readers to contain an unnecessary degree of self-pity, but to me it does not.

Comment. It is a long Letter, but now I am conscious of its importance, I think it worthy of the space.

NOVEMBER NEWS ITEMS

Colour TV is inching closer. Test Patterns will be started in September, and transmission will begin in March.

The unions have an **oft-quoted policy of "one man, one job".** But the **Prime Minister's wife currently has four jobs**, including writing a diary for *Woman's Day*....

"Please explain", say the Press.

In NSW, the State Government is debating whether to **allow Sunday Trading by hotels.** At the moment, the vote is split about 50-50. There should be a decision within a few weeks.

The Australian Government entered into agreement with **two mining companies to allow them to mine, and export, uranium from the Northern Territory**.... Since then the States and Territories and the Australian Government have **flip-flopped on their policies to allow mining and export.** At the moment, **none of them allow** the use of uranium **for production of electricity within Australia.** Many of them do allow mining and export.

The United Nations just avoided expelling South Africa from its ranks. This was because it was persisting with its policy of apartheid, and because it was refusing Namibia independence....

Australia voted **to expel** South Africa. Britain and the US voted to **not** do so....

The question has been raised as to whether Australia is thus **interfering in the internal affairs of another country.**

Some readers will remember when **travelling shows** visited suburbs and country towns once a year, and stopped a few nights with hirdy-girdies and side-shows and tents. **One feature was always a boxing tent**, where local lads were paid to fight among themselves or against the tent's rough and tumble "professionals"....

An eighteen-year-old lad in Victoria accepted the challenge, and was knocked down twice. He later **collapsed and died** because of the beating he took. The prize that the boy fought for was **Four Pounds**, a trifle....

The Victorian Government says that it **will ban all boxing tents in the future.**

NSW, and other States, are moving to stop hitch-hiking because of increasing crime rates associated with it.

In the US, in the first Congressional mid-term elections since Nixon resigned, **the Democrats had a landslide,** though the Republican Ford will remain as President for another two years.

A 17-year-old Sydney lad has been **refused a school reference** because he **would not wear a school uniform** for his last two years at his school.

PUBS OPEN ON SUNDAYS

Here we are again answering the question of should pubs open on Sunday. The timing varies from State to State, but about five years ago the question was answered by referenda in the various States. This time round, it seems that existing **Parliaments** might make the decision.

In any case, you can be certain that if it is legalised in one State, then the others will soon follow, in a year or two.

So, the arguments are being revived and sent to print.

This writer, below, provides a single Letter that more or less summarises what the arguments are. I thank him for saving me that trouble.

Letters, J Stewart. It appears from Saturday Forum that all hell will break loose with the Sunday opening of hotels. There will be unparalleled carnage on the roads, family life will suffer, the economy will be disrupted and, according to one correspondent, "Mr Maddison will soon be extending the size of the police force to chase drunks."

Another correspondent foresees increased pub brawls, absenteeism on Mondays and even an attempt to change the Lord's Prayer to "**My** will be done," whatever that means.

Yet another writer believes that "the beer barons of NSW" have nurtured the idea that tourists want a drink on Sundays, and hopes that the electors will not be deprived of a democratic vote, "in view of such a recent rejection." In fact, the "rejection" by the electors was five years ago and was by a little more than half of them. What about the other half?

We are not children and the great majority of drinkers are not no-hopers. Let those who like a drink in their leisure time have one, and let those who don't want to, mind their own business.

Comment. All indications so far suggest that **this time** the "open" camp will win. Of course, the Churches are campaigning against this. And the dedicated anti-liquor groups. But they do not appear to be making as much progress as in the past. It could be that our population is becoming more attuned to looking at the Western world, and is accepting of its habits.

In any case, if I was betting, I would say that in NSW, by referendum or by Parliament whichever, the pubs will "open" soon on Sundays.

OZ BEEF FOR AUSTRALIANS

Letters, J Robinson. I hope that every shopper in Sydney has taken advantage of the beautiful rump steak surprisingly available in Sydney as a bonus result of the lack of international buyers.

Also I hope that some decisive move will be made by the correct authority to keep enough export-quality beef in Australia for Australians - permanently. I have read that even the best rump was sent to the Americans to mince up for hamburgers. It is incredible to me that we had to put up with tough, low-fat, flavourless grilling steak in this country, while our Japanese friends were enjoying this wonderful mature beef of ours - and probably cut up into strips for sukyaki.

I and my family had never seen the like of the wonderful rump steak which I bought for 69c a lb at Wynyard two weeks ago. I bought so much that we are still enjoying it.

Comment. I think that most of us agree with this sentiment. We are sympathetic towards our primary producers, **but** it is true that as soon as a market overseas becomes profitable, the prices here rise and the best of the produce is sent to other countries.

Personal comment. From this grieving lobster-eater: "Here Here."

TWO WEEKS OF WHITLAM'S WOES

About the middle of November, Whitlam had a particularly hard trot. All of the following problems came to goad him over a ten-day period.

Trade Deficit. The figures for the September quarter show that Australia had a **record trade deficit of $620 million**. This type of bad news is accumulating, and it is obvious that someone in authority has to recognise this....

Who will be the first person to spell it out to the Australian public?

Pilots strike. The nation was full of cries from anyone in authority for **restraint in demanding and granting of wage increases.** But, the Tribunal for fixing the remuneration of **airline pilots granted them an increase of 29 per cent per annum....**

"Outrage" was the universal cry. How could a Government body affix its stamp to such an increase? Even the Minister for Labour and Industry foresaw "the questioning of the concept of wage justice".

Headline news. The October employment figures showed a jump of 24 per cent in unemployment from the previous month....

Also it was announced that 500 people at Ford Motor Company would be dismissed....

The Head of Bradmill, Australia's largest cotton manufacturer, said 1,100 workers had been dismissed....

Bob Hawke steps in. The head of the ACTU, Bob Hawke, told the Prime Minister that it would be political lunacy to wait until Christmas before addressing the economic problems.

Tax relief. The Prime Minister, and Treasurer Crean, announced new relieving measures for the taxpayer. These included tax cuts of about three percent, and small decreases in company taxes. Crean also will give some protection to the car industry, and a small relaxation of the credit squeeze....

He hopefully said that he expected the Unions **to accept the tax cuts as a substitute for wage increases** when they came before Wage Tribunals in the future. Union leaders were not so keen on this.

Crean and Cairns swap. Many of Whitlam's Cabinet were being fractious, sometimes openly criticising policy, or even Whitlam himself. He had persevered with Crean as Treasurer for too long, and now the chips were down, he decided that Crean and Jim Cairns should swap portfolios. Neither of these wanted the change, so this added to those in Cabinet who were not at all happy....

But it did put a new Minister, Cairns, in charge of Treasury. Maybe he could do something with that institution that might stimulate the economy. He certainly said he could. Maybe he was right.

Comment. That was a lot of bad news within a fortnight. A mere mortal might have been crushed by it all. But a mere mortal Whitlam was not. So he escaped the crusher.

THE LIBERALS WERE ALSO RESTLESS

The Opposition, led by the Liberal Party, were not making any headway. This was seen by some of the Parliamentary Members as not satisfactory. Surely, they argued, with all the problems that were publicly discussed at the moment, the Liberal Party should be able to capitalise on Labor's problems, but that was not happening.

The Leader of the Opposition was Mr Snedden, who was a moderate person, perhaps not well suited to the fiery atmosphere in the House at the moment. In any case, a faction in the Party **badly** planned a coup to displace him. This coup failed by a ratio of two to one.

It showed, however, that there was a significant number of rebels, and that perhaps a better-organised attempt might be successful. We will keep an eye on this.

Incidentally, the nominee to take Mr Snedden's place was a Mr Malcolm Fraser. He took no active role in the attempted coup, and expressed his support for Mr Snedden after it.

TAX BENEFITS

The Government announced earlier this month that some Tax benefits would be passed on to taxpayers. They included that **interest paid on home loans would be tax deductible**. That sounds nice to me if I have a mortgage. But what if I do not?

Letters, R House, Director, The Phillips and House Group. The Federal Labor decision to make interest on home-purchase loans deductible from income for tax purposes seems anti-social, quite stupid and inflationary.

It is anti-social because it results in the poorest section of our people, the rentpayers, bearing an increased share of the tax burden compared with their more fortunate peers who are buying homes.

It is stupid because it will not really help home buyers but will result in an enormous rise in the price of land and houses as the pressure to buy is greatly increased.

It is inflationary because it represents a release of more money into the economy by reducing the Commonwealth Budget surplus or increasing the deficit.

Altogether an amazing decision from representatives of a party claiming a special concern for the welfare of the poor.

Letters, P Brewer. This is not to say that there should not be sympathy for persons paying off their homes, but such tax rebates would merely reduce the common taxation pool and therefore have to be supported by other taxpayers.

Why should a young couple unable to buy their own home, and therefore forced to pay rent, be put in a position of being virtually obliged to subsidise those more fortunate than themselves?

The same applies to persons who have already paid off their homes **without tax concessions in past years**.

The proposal is typical of the half-baked thinking which has characterised the Labor Government since it came into office in December, 1972.

Tax relief is long overdue but it should, as Mr Snedden has proposed, benefit the whole range of taxpayers and not merely a favoured section.

One writer bemoans the fact that a **new** Capital Gains tax will be introduced. He says that it has not caused much resentment as yet because it is not **immediately** payable. It will only become so when an asset is sold. That could be years away, but it certainly will be paid at some stage.

Another writer says that the Capital Gains tax should be indexed. That is, as inflation increases, the apparent value of an asset, its real value, decreases. Unless the value of the asset is indexed, then the CGT will tax people on what is really a fall in value.

A third writer says that indexation should apply to the **entire** taxation scale.

Comment. Voters are pretty astute. When you examine the taxation concessions granted, they were not much at all. And there were catches all over them. As they gradually happen, they will become nails in the coffin for the present Government.

AMATEUR RADIO

In 1974, without many computers, it was possible to communicate from any person to any person via **amateur radio**. Both parties needed radio wave receivers and transmitters, both needed to be licensed, and have their own unique call sign. A set-up such as this was often called ham radio, and was used to send messages between friends, to talk to business associates, and often to send warnings of impending events, or emergency messages.

Its use in Australia was mainly for messages between clusters of operators who would set up in the evenings to chat to other operators. Most of them were "hammers" who loved the whole operation, and were great enthusiasts for what they saw as a hobby. A number of hammers set themselves up in special rooms, often called "shacks", and that name has found its way into 2024 usage.

Alas, inevitably, there were a few problems. See below.

Letters, G Stern. I wish to express my complete and utter surprise at the Federal Government's Budget decision to increase the licence fees for radio amateurs by 100 per cent (from $6 to $12). Customs duty and sales tax had raised the price of equipment to unrealistic levels, although amateur radio provides a community service (eg, in the recent Brisbane floods).

Radio amateurs have to sit for a difficult examination (pass mark 70 per cent), pay for the privilege to sit for the exam and, if passed, pay for their station licence yearly. Their purchases are taxed, their privileges are limited, and public relations are poor.

An example of bad public relations is the case of radio pirates. If the case of a person illegally operating a radio station is recorded in the newspapers, he is invariably called a radio amateur. Amateur radio itself barely rates a mention in the press.

I wish to make a plea to the Herald and all its readers. Write to your local member and suggest that tariffs on amateur radio equipment be abolished. Some day it may be your life which may not be saved because some radio amateur could not afford new equipment.

Comment. Despite government regulations, the number of "hammers" of course **increased** during the World Wars as people were desperate for overseas news that came on the air. With the advent of computers, and then rapid growth of the Internet since the Eighties, the number has fallen right down again.

But there are still enthusiasts who club together for exchanging information and greetings.

IN PRAISE OF PRIVET

Earlier we looked at the benefits of lantana. Now it seems that farmers and city dwellers alike are anxious to expose the humble privet as villain number one.

A dozen Letters have been published by the Herald over a month, and if you believe them, the privet as a hedge, or in some other form, is a nuisance par excellence.

But, as usual, someone disagrees.

Letters, L Johnson. The pollen from this much maligned shrub or tree - in my case beautiful trees - is always being blamed for causing hay fever and asthma. If this is a medically proven fact, which I doubt, may I inquire how the relatively short flowering period of approximately two to three weeks can pollute the air with enough pollen to cause the continuation of these complaints during the rest of the year.

My lovely trees not only are frequented by happy bees, but give me shade and privacy and, during their flowering, many hours of real delight in regarding their graceful branches laden with millions of tiny flowers - a truly fairy-like effect.

This they do year after year, receiving no attention whatsoever in return, other than my grateful thanks. And for this I should destroy them? Never.

HITCH-HIKING IS OK

Students were probably the main hitch-hikers in the nation. So it is not surprising that Letters from student bodies were in all the Papers.

Letters, S Sanders, Macquarie University. It is somewhat disturbing to read of the State Government's intentions of "getting tough" with hitch-hikers. Leaving aside the dubious assumption that not only children, but also mature adults, need to be protected from themselves, there remains the question of what are the alternatives to hitch-hiking? For many people the answer is simple - there are none.

The simple fact is that most hitch-hikers are either too young or too poor to drive cars, and are invariably faced with a public transport service that is either non-existent or infrequent, slow, noisy or dirty. For this service (or lack of it) passengers are asked to pay fares which can best be described as prohibitive.

Under these circumstances, it is no wonder that many people see no alternative to hitch-hiking.

To provide them with one, Mr Morris, and his Government, will need to make a concerted effort to improve public transport, instead of wasting the taxpayers' money on cart-before-the-horse anti-hitch-hiking programs and obsolete radial expressway systems. Unless this is done, the present State Government may well go down in history as the one which immobilised the poor and choked the city of Sydney in its own exhaust fumes.

Comment. The various moves to deter getting a free ride were successful. After a number of years in the past when the most atrocious crimes were committed on motorists, it was fairly easy to persuade motorists to abandon the practice of picking up strangers.

I add that the crimes were not in general committed by students. But they shared in the feeling of fear in the general public.

AN ARGUMENT FOR BATTERIES IN CARS

Letters, F Laws. The threatened world-wide shortage of petrol brings to mind an interesting question: why have **cars driven by electric batteries** not been improved appreciably?

About 50 years ago a man (I think he managed a music shop in the City) used to drive along Goulburn Street between his home and the City in a battery-powered car.

At that time also I knew a man named Allen in Sussex Street, City, who sold batteries, and he used to deliver them in a battery-driven utility. I can recall seeing two rows of batteries in his utility, one row for sale and the other to drive the utility.

The battery-driven vehicle at that time had one outstanding disadvantage; the batteries had to be changed or recharged every 40 or 50 miles, and 50 miles is nowadays a very small distance.

Alternatively, a ton or so of batteries would be needed to drive the car 500 miles.

If the brains who improved the petrol-driven vehicle got together, we might well get perhaps 500 miles instead of 50 from battery-driven cars.

Batteries can be charged from **a dynamo powered by a steam engine**. Steam could be produced from coal and water, of which we have ample supplies in Australia.

Furthermore, in many cases the batteries could be charged at home at night when the call for electric power for major purposes is at a minimum.

I hope that someone who knows more about this subject than I do will take some action.

LOSING TEACHERS

In all States, there was a big percentage of public school teachers who were resigning their positions.

Letters, P Cramer. The Victorian Minister for Education has shown that he is totally unaware of his numbers. Any reasonable employer who lost 13.5 per cent of his employees through resignation in one year would set about trying to find out why and, having done so, would try to eliminate, as far as possible, the causes of discontent.

It is the incoming Premier's task to appoint as Minister for Education a man with the vision to review the reasons for low morale and who will take a positive approach to improving the conditions under which teachers work. That way, the resignation rate will be reduced and some of the many thousands of teachers may be induced to re-enter the teaching profession for which they were trained.

Comment. Shades of 2024.

DECEMBER NEWS ITEMS

Dr Jim Cairns has now become Treasurer. He has chosen his office staff, and among these is **Miss Juni Morosi.** Her job will be Office Co-ordinator. Opposition Members claimed **that the Attorney-General had improperly** tried to get her low-rent accommodation....

Also, it was alleged by Mr John Howard (Liberal) that she was **perhaps linked to a company under investigation in NSW. This proved to be spurious**, but it was hardly a welcome to Cairns's staff....

Morosi will become newsworthy soon.

Remember **in 1974** when the **bread carter delivered bread daily to your home.** Now that system is under challenge. **Supermarkets are offering lower prices to housewives,** and that is taking business away from the carters....

If the 'markets are successful, then that will mean **the end of home delivery of bread. Can you imagine a world without that?**

First week-end in December. In the **Queensland State elections**, the Liberal Government was returned to power in a **staggering swing against Labor** in the State elections....

The Opposition leader and his Deputy (both Labor) were both ousted....

The number of seats that Labor now holds has been **reduced from 33 to 12....**

The number of unemployed rose by 41,000 to 190,000 in November. That rise is enormous....

Is it time to panic yet, Gough?

The *Sydney Morning Herald's* **Sunday paper** now has circulation of **680,000 copies per week.**

Mr Whitlam has a plan to travel overseas on a five week tour. Bob Hawke now proposes that he cancel that trip, because of the economic problems that the nation faces....

Whitlam says he has no thought of doing that, because it **would be"rude" to the leaders of other countries** to do so....

Hawke said "it's not much use in him becoming a celebrity overseas if **he loses his Prime Ministership at home".**

Juni Morosi gave her first Press Conference to a packed audience of 50 male and female journalists. **She denied "sexual innuendoes" about her relationships with Ministers Cairns and Murphy.**

Amid this drama, the *SMH* reporter, on **the front page of the** *Herald*, reported that "she was wearing a white cotton dress with a gold charm, with a green jade pendant on it, and toe-peeper shoes"....

Miss Morosi remained cool and composed during a long 10-minute interview with a news-hungry Press.

FOOD FOR THE WORLD'S STARVING

Conferences were being held around the world talking about the problem of starvation amid the poorer nations. US Secretary of State, Henry Kissinger, was at the forefront among these. The general tenor was that more gifts of free food should be given to these countries.

Letters, M Barlow. What a hollow facade the UN World Food Conference presents with Dr Kissinger making flamboyant statements about increasing the production and distribution of world food supplies.

The same could be said for our Freedom from Hunger Campaign and Austcare organisations. It seems that the predictions of the authors of Famine 75 are going to come true unless we do something drastic about **the basic problem which is overpopulation**.

How can we justify giving food to people who, when asked how their 13 children will survive, reply: "Allah will provide"?

I, for one, will not give a cent to any organisation supplying nutritional relief without a related policy of population control, but would welcome and strongly support a "Freedom from People-Pollution" campaign aimed at supplying and administering birth-control devices, abortion and sterilisation programs in conjunction with food handouts.

But this Letter brought a reaction.

Letters, A Burton. Before refusing to give a cent to relieve the starvation of other human beings, has M Barlow inquired what proportion of such aid goes to people with 13 children who rely on the providence of Allah?

In the past, these people have learned that large families are a necessity because of the appalling child mortality rate. The children who survive are needed to help provide a living for the family and to care for the parents in their old age. This custom cannot be changed overnight and any "Freedom from People Pollution" campaign Mr Barlow would support can only be a very long-range project.

In the meantime, hundreds of thousands of men, women and children are dying largely because of terrible droughts over which they have no control. Perhaps Mr Barlow might like to ponder this as he sits in his no-doubt comfortable home after a wholesome dinner, before watching television. Perhaps he might then decide he could spare a little after all.

Comment. It appears to me that Mr Burton missed the thrust of Mr Barlow's Letter. I think this was asking for **ways of reducing the birth rate** of afflicted nations through some concerted effort to stop the population increase in the first place.

But both writers were rightly concerned about the starvation in some nations. It is a matter which has persisted, and for which no **world-wide** solution has been found.

TOUGH ON THE LAND

Our farmers and graziers were not being spared from tough conditions. The Federal Government was aware of this, and announced a series of loans to the various industries. The terms of the loans were generous, with smallish interest rates, and a moderate repayment over a long term.

Opposition Ministers as usual said the loans were too little, too late. But the loans were of help to some, and at least showed that some Ministries inside the Government were aware of the reality of what was facing the nation.

THREE SUGGESTIONS FROM WRITERS

Christmas is almost here, and the Press cuts down on the headlines bemoaning tough times. Even the Letters Pages change to a measure of goodwill, and criticisms of the Government changed to good suggestions on how we can make the world a better place.

Letters, G Mayo-Jaffray. The Australian Government has announced that rates of tax on earnings are to be reduced for the 1974/75 financial year and that a double reduction in PAYE instalments is to apply for the second six months, from January, 1975.

It has also announced that the reduced tax deduction cannot be put into effect for several weeks after that initially projected date, because of governmental administrative difficulties.

I suggest that the Government now issues a direction to all employers that no tax instalments be deducted from employees' salaries and wages for the payday immediately prior to Christmas. Such a gesture would considerably help most families at this time of additional expense and would be in line with the Government's pledge of assistance through tax relief.

Letters, R Stuart. Everyone most surely agree with the eulogistic comments of Mrs E Killen apropos Taronga Zoo. And let us hope that her worthy suggestions will spur the board to even further praiseworthy achievements.

One imperative improvement would be the procurement of a liquor licence for the quaint old refreshment rooms. When I recently escorted a small group of visiting South American friends to the zoo, we were all horrified to find that it was not possible to order a glass of wine or even a humble noggin of beer with our lunch.

Letters, L Wilson. What can be done about the "Dodgem" of the road?

I refer to the many Sydney taxidrivers who remove their chrome bumper protection and replace this with the impervious protection of a thick piece of sprung steel, both in the front and at the rear of their vehicles. Confident that they cannot be harmed by others, they then drive with abandon, changing lanes at will, and "throwing out the anchors" if they detect a hail from the corner of their eye, secure in the knowledge that if they are hit from behind, not only is it the other fellow's fault, but that he will come off a very second best.

Worse still is the situation when the careless "dodgem" driver cannons into the rear of some unsuspecting motorist who has not had the forethought to modify his car to gain adequate protection. Admittedly it is, in this case, the taxidriver's fault, but guess who has suffered most.

CHRISSIE PRESENTS FOR DAD

What to buy for Christmas? This year, for a change, I will give **Dad** a break.

Richards Store brings festive cheer to the man in your life, with all the handsome goodies he goes for.

Pure silk, pure luxury in imported **English foulard dressing gowns**, richly beautiful as only **pure silk** can be in a variety of spots in navy/gold, navy/red, red/black or jacquard design navy/red or navy/gold, $72 or plain silk shantung in red or royal at $65. **Foulard**

pyjamas by 'Bonsoir' of London in pure 'Macclesfield' silks in pastel shades of biscuit, sky or rich royal blue $55.

Ties to delight him from contemporary to traditional, Richards have them all! Hand-made English foulards in colours and patterns to amaze the eye. From $9. Handsome richly woven silks from London - handmade in neat or bold patterns, $15. **Bow ties are back...** pure silk foulard prints from London in neats and spots $6. Knitted silk ties from 'Holiday & Brown' in wine, chocolate, fawn or grey $15.

Fine cotton **knitted sports shirts** from 'Smedley' of England. There is nothing to compare with **Smedley's soft Sea Island cotton** half sleeve sports shirts, or **long sleeved polo neck skivvies** with their fully fashioned sleeves in white, bone, yellow, coffee, navy, sky or red $15 for either the shirt or the skivvies.

DISASTER IN DARWIN

Early on Christmas Day, the city of Darwin was destroyed by Cyclone Tracy. In a city of only 41,000, 44 people were soon reported as dead, and 20,000 were homeless. Thousands of houses were destroyed, city buildings were shattered, military bases were knocked out completely. Water and therefore sewage were not available, likewise food, electricity, medical services. Hospitals were flooded, and morgues, and roadways were lost. **I could go on.**

As an immediate response, 20,000 people were trying to evacuate Darwin. All air transport had been destroyed, and the airport was hopeless. Communications were all gone. So evacuation was fraught with difficulties.

The news shocked the nation on this Christmas Day. **There were no flipant "Merry Christmas" greetings in 1974.** Much of the nation was concerned with how it could help. "In every way possible", was the answer. **Which, I am happy to say, it did.**

For the entire nation, Tracy was a terrible way to end the year.

SUMMARISING 1974

Despite all the bad news raging across the nation, Christmas preparations appeared normal. Lots of parties, shopping, presents, lunches, noisy children, women fainting in crowds, a bit of booze.

But behind the joviality, **no one could ignore that this nation had seen its fortunes drop badly** in the last half year. And into Christmas. I spared you the details of the end-of-year continuing disappointments, but they **did** continue on into December. There was no sign of the light at the end of the tunnel.

Even Gough Whitlam said in late December that 1974 had been the worst year in 45 years. **That takes us back to the start of the Depression, a startling admission.**

I will not go back over all the depressing news that I have been spinning out over the last few months. But I will add that it is hard to see, at the end of 1974, that the nation **next year** will be any better off financially, that our Government will pull itself together, and that people will be more secure and happy.

I wish I could say, as I have done year-after-year in the past, that this has been a happy year for the nation. **I wish it were true** that I could forecast that next year, and the year after, would be even better. But I cannot do this.

The best I can muster is **the wish that the nation will recover soon**, and all will be right again. But, my fingers are firmly crossed, and I have figuratively written that in invisible ink.

Still, there is some hope. We have a nation of good people with a more-or-less common purpose, and a good knowledge of what's right. **In the long run, this nation will emerge from its coming doldrums.** I just hope it is sooner rather than later.

COMMENTS FROM READERS

Tom Lynch, Spears Point.....Some history writers make the mistake of trying to boost their authority by including graphs and charts all over the place. You on the other hand get a much better effect by saying things like "he made a pile". Or "every one worked hours longer that they should have, and felt like death warmed up at the end of the shift." I have seen other writers waste two pages of statistics painting the same picture as you did in a few words....

Barry Marr, Adelaide....you know that I am being facetious when I say that I wish the war had gone on for years longer so that you would have written more books about it...

Edna College, Auburn.... A few times I stopped and sobbed as you brought memories of the postman delivering letters, and the dread that ordinary people felt as he neared. How you captured those feelings yet kept your coverage from becoming maudlin or bogged down is a wonder to me....

Betty Kelly. Every time you seem to be getting serious you throw in a phrase or memory that lightens up the mood. In particular, in the war when you were describing the terrible carnage of Russian troops, you ended with a ten line description of how aggrieved you felt and ended it with "apart from that, things are pretty good here". For me, it turned the unbearable into the bearable, and I went from feeling morbid and angry back to a normal human being....

Alan Davey, Brisbane....I particularly liked the light-hearted way you described the scenes at the airports as the American high-flying entertainers flew in. I had always seen the crowd behaviour as disgraceful, but your light-hearted description of it made me realise it was in fact harmless and just good fun.

MORE INFORMATION ON THESE BOOKS

Over the past 16 years the author, Ron Williams, has written this series of books that present a social history of Australia in the post-war period. They cover the period for 1939 to 1974, with one book for each year. Thus there are 36 books.

To capture the material for each book, the author, Ron Williams, worked his way through the *Sydney Morning Herald* and *The Age/Argus* day-by-day, and picked out the best stories, ideas and trivia. He then wrote them up into 180 pages of a year-book.

He writes in a direct conversational style, he has avoided statistics and charts, and has produced easily-read material that is entertaining, and instructive, and charming.

They are invaluable as gifts for birthdays, Christmas, and anniversaries, and for the oldies who are hard to buy for.

These books are available at all good book stores and newsagents. They are listed also in all leading catalogues, including Title Page and Dymocks and Booktopia.

THERE ARE 36 TITLES IN THIS SERIES
For the 36 years from 1939 to 1974

Chrissie and birthday books for Mum and Dad and Aunt and Uncle and cousins and family and friends and work and everyone else.

Don't forget a good read and chuckle for yourself.

In 1953, pets in churches were welcomed with open arms. Painless childbirth was popular, especially among women. Be warned - the coronation of Elizabeth will soon be in the news. Edmund Hillary reached the top. Thallium became popular, as a footballer found out. Lots of Pom migrants had done their time, and went back to Mother England.

In 1954, Queen Elizabeth II was sent here victorious, and Petrov was our very own spy - what a thrill. Boys were being sentenced to life. Johnny Ray cried all the way to the bank. Church halls were being used for dirty dancing. Open the pubs after six? Were they ever shut? A-bombs had scaredies scared.

In 1955, be careful of the demon drink, get your brand new Salk injections, submit your design for the Sydney Opera house now, prime your gelignite for another Redex Trial, and stop your greyhounds killing cats. Princess Margaret shocked the Church, Huxley shocked the Bishops, and our Sundays are far from shocking.

AVAILABLE AT ALL GOOD BOOKSTORES
AND NEWSAGENTS

In 1956, the first big issue was the Suez crisis, which put our own Bob Menzies on the world stage, but he got no applause. TV was turned on in time for the Melbourne Olympics, Hungary was invaded and the Iron Curtain got a lot thicker. There was much concern about cruelty to sharks, and the horrors of country pubs persisted.

In 1957, Britain's Red Dean said Chinese Reds were OK. America avoided balance-of-payments problems by sending entertainers here. Sydney's Opera House will use lotteries to raise funds. The Russians launched Sputnik and a dog got a free ride. A bodkin crisis shook the nation.

In 1958, the Christian brothers bought a pub and raffled it; some clergy thought that Christ would not be pleased. Circuses were losing animals at a great rate. Officials were in hot water because the Queen Mother wasn't given a sun shade; it didn't worry the lined-up school children, they just fainted as normal. School milk was hot news, bread home deliveries were under fire. The RSPCA was killing dogs in a gas chamber. A tribe pointed the bone at Albert Namatjira; he died soon after.

www.ingramcontent.com/pod-product-compliance
Lightning Source LLC
Chambersburg PA
CBHW041257040426
42334CB00028BA/3052